Captivating

A Guided Journal to Aid in
Unveiling the Mystery of a Woman's Soul

By John and Stasi Eldredge

Nelson Impact
A Division of Thomas Nelson Publishers
Since 1798

www.thomasnelson.com

OTHER BOOKS BY JOHN ELDREDGE

The Sacred Romance
(Coauthored with Brent Curtis)

The Journey of Desire

Wild at Heart

Waking the Dead

Epic

To my friend Sam,
Who so unabashedly dives into matters of the heart.

Published by Nelson Impact, a Division of Thomas Nelson, Inc., P.O. Box 141000, Nashville, Tennessee, 37214.

Published in association with Yates & Yates, LLP, Attorneys and Counselors, Orange, California.

Printed in the United States of America

05 06 07 08 09 RRD 9 8 7 6 5 4 3

Introduction

Welcome and well done! Choosing to purchase this "guided journal" means that you are hungry for more. More of God, more healing, and more restoration into the woman you were created to be. It says that you are willing to take a journey of discovery *with him.* You have said "yes" to God. You are continuing to say "yes." May he meet you in the deep places of your heart and bring you hope, courage, healing, and the delights of intimacy that only God can bring.

First, this is not your normal "workbook." There are no wrong answers. No fill-in-the-blanks. You don't have to struggle or worry about "getting it right." Who wants another workbook anyway? We have enough work to do already. Besides, calling this a workbook would imply that the messages in the book *Captivating* are to be mastered. And mastered in a measurable way. Not at all. The messages in the book are to be pondered, considered. Some embraced. Some practiced. Some set aside for a later time.

This journal is for your heart.

And words are the voice of the heart.

The excerpts from the book and the questions we ask are here simply to provoke further exploration of your own heart and the heart of God. The pages provided allow space for your soul to express what lies within. Don't edit yourself. These pages are for you and God alone. If you choose to journey with other women in a small group, share what you desire. You don't need to be afraid of getting it wrong or saying something stupid. We really are in this thing together. It's amazing how much in common we have in our experiences, our feelings, our doubts, our fears.

Within each chapter, we have included special features called "Windows to the Heart" and "Lifting the Veil." These include excerpts from other books and movies as well as side notes that we wanted to include but couldn't fit in the companion book, *Captivating*. We hope you enjoy them and that they are helpful in your journey with God.

If you are using this little book to facilitate deeper conversations, don't try to answer all of the questions together in one gathering. Three or four will be enough. React. Respond. Share honestly. Take the risk of being vulnerable with one another. A covenant of privacy will help. Decide together that what is shared within the confines of your gathering is sacred and not to be shared with others.

Providing a haven where one's heart is welcomed to show up is a great gift. Your heart *is* wanted. Whether you are using this journal alone, with God, or with a group of women and God, allow room for your heart to show up. Quiet yourself. Relax. Invite the Holy Spirit to guide you, speak to you, reveal what he desires to reveal.

The invitation is a true one. It is from God. And it is ever before you to come more fully into his presence and know him. Know yourself. And become ever more you, ever more his.

All of us are on a journey whether we know it or not. A journey of becoming. Henri Nouwen writes in *The Life of the Beloved* that, "the spiritual life is not simply a way of being, but also a way of becoming." May God use this book in your life to aid you in becoming the woman you truly are. May he draw near to you as you draw near to him. Ask him to come. And rest assured that he will for, indeed, he has promised to do so; he delights in coming.

—Stasi Eldredge

For Zion's sake I will not keep silent,
for Jerusalem's sake I will not remain quiet,
till her righteousness shines out like the dawn [until you shimmer],
her salvation like a blazing torch.
The nations will see your righteousness,
and all kings your glory [your beauty];
you will be called by a new name
that the mouth of the LORD will bestow.
You will be a crown of splendor in the LORD's hand [the crown of creation],
a royal diadem in the hand of your God.
No longer will they call you Deserted,
or name your land Desolate.
But you will be called Hephzibah, and your land Beulah
for the LORD will take delight in you, and your land will be married.
As a young man marries a maiden [he pursues her, romances her]
So will your sons marry you;
as a bridegroom rejoices over his bride [you are lovely],
so will your God rejoice over you.

—IS. 62:1–5 NKJV

CHAPTER ONE

The Heart of a Woman

Sometimes it's hard to be a woman.
—TAMMY WYNETTE

You belong among the wildflowers
You belong in a boat out at sea
You belong with your love on your arm
You belong somewhere you feel free.
—TOM PETTY, "WILDFLOWERS"

I love the sentence "Sometimes, it's hard to be a woman" from the old Tammy Wynette song. Talk about an understatement. Yes, there are many, many times when it is very hard to be a man as well. Yet, we women are living at a time when the pressures from without and the pressures from within to live well as a woman often feel massive and relentless. Sometimes, it's *harder* to be a woman.

Welcome, Beloved of God. Take a deep breath. Relax. You are among friends here. Before you pick up a pen, take a moment to invite Jesus into your time now; ask Him to guide and lead and have his way with your thoughts and your heart. He is after all, the creator of our hearts, as women. He knows who we are. He knows and understands the stories of our lives much better than we do. And he knows the desires of our hearts with intimate detail. He placed them there. Let's ask him to come and to help us.

Dear Jesus, I love you. I need you. I come before you now, once again, as yours, asking for your help, your grace. My life is yours. My heart is yours. Would you please come and shine your light into the depths of my heart that I might understand myself better and come to know your healing and your presence more deeply. Help me to remember what I need to remember. Help me to see, to understand, to repent, to forgive and to become. Jesus, I give you access to all of my heart. I invite you into every part. Come, Holy Spirit, have your way—that I might love you, God, more deeply and truly with all of my heart, soul, mind, and strength. In Jesus' name I pray. Amen.

Windows to Your Heart

John and I love movies, because they speak so deeply to the heart. (You'll remember that Jesus loved to tell stories, too. He did it to reach the heart.) In chapter one of the companion book we said, "Look at the games that little girls play, and if you can, remember what you dreamed of as a little girl. Look at the movies women love. Listen to your own heart and the hearts of the women you know. What is it that a woman wants? What does she dream of?" It might be really helpful, as a way of entering into this journey, to go back and watch one or two of your favorite movies. And as you do, ask yourself, Why do I love this? What does it stir in me?

In fact, why don't you jot down the names of several movies you love right here:

The Notebook.
old movie - The promise
The vow

Now, as you begin, flip back over chapter one in *Captivating* and skim the pages. Did you highlight anything? What strikes you? What did it evoke in your heart?

The old woman at Christmas time wearing the Christmas dress and feeling pretty, twirling around. "Timeless Beauty".

Thought about the contrast to Jan's life. Being Amish/Men and Beauty was something to be ashamed of.

What do you like about this chapter?

What do you not like about it? What are you struggling with?

What, if anything presented in this chapter, are you having a hard time believing?

Coming Alive

I began chapter one in the companion book by retelling the story of our Oxbow Bend canoeing experience; the beauty of it and the dangerous turn it took.

> We rose to the challenge working together, and the fact that it required all of me, that I was in it with my family and for my family, that I was surrounded by wild, shimmering beauty and it was, well, kind of dangerous made the time . . . transcendent.

A Woman's Journey

Have you experienced something similar? Can you recall a time in your life when you felt *alive* as a woman? Who were you with? What happened? How did you feel?

Then the time came when the risk
it took
To remain tight in a bud was more
painful
Than the risk it took to blossom.

—Anais Nin

When did you first know that you were no longer a girl, but had become a woman, a "grown up"? Was there a milestone? An event?

Do you feel like you *are* a woman? Are there places in your heart where you still feel young?

There seems to be a growing number of books on the masculine journey—rites of passage, initiations, and the like—many of them helpful. But there has been precious little wisdom offered on the path to becoming a woman. Oh, we know the expectations that have been laid upon us by our families, our churches, and our cultures. There are reams of materials on what you ought to do to be a good woman. But that is not the same thing as knowing what the journey towards becoming a woman involves, or even what the goal really should be.

What expectations have been laid upon you, as a woman? What do you feel the pressure to be?

perfect mom.
perfect kids - college, great job.
always in control.

The church has not been a big help here. No, that's not quite honest enough. The church has been part of the problem. Its message to women has been primarily "you are here to serve. That's why God created you: to serve. In the nursery, in the kitchen, on various committees, in your home, in your community." Seriously now—picture the women we hold up as models of femininity in the church. They are sweet, they are helpful, their hair is coiffed; they are busy, they are disciplined, they are composed, and they are *tired.*

Think about the women you meet at church. They're trying to live up to some model of femininity. What do they "teach" you about being a woman? What are they saying to us through their lives?

They are selfless -
Dont have lives outside of husbands/fam.
are always secondary to husbands
(dont out talk them)

What have you been taught that a mature, godly woman should look like?

Unseen, Unsought, and Uncertain

I know I am not alone in this nagging sense of failing to measure up, a feeling of not being good enough as a woman. Every woman I've ever met feels it—something deeper than just the sense of failing at what she does. An underlying, gut feeling of failing at who she *is. I am not enough,* and, *I am too much,* at the same time.

Have you ever felt that way? Are you feeling it these days? In what ways?

not being a perfect mother.
not having perfect kids.
not being thin.

The result is Shame, the universal companion of women. It haunts us, nipping at our heels, feeding on our deepest fear that we will end up abandoned and alone.

After all, if we were better women—whatever *that* means—life wouldn't be so hard. Right?

Do you believe that? That if you were "better" life wouldn't be so hard? "Better" in what ways?

Why is it so hard to create meaningful friendships and sustain them? Why do our days seem so unimportant, filled not with romance and adventure but with duties and demands? We feel unseen, even by those who are closest to us. We feel *unsought*—that no one has the passion or the courage to pursue us, to get past our messiness to find the woman deep inside. And we feel *uncertain*—uncertain what it even means to be a woman; uncertain what it truly means to be feminine; uncertain if we are or ever will be.

Do you feel like you know what it means to be a true woman? Do you feel like you are?

Aware of our deep failings, we pour contempt on our own hearts for wanting more. Oh, we long for intimacy and for adventure; we long to be the Beauty of some great story. But the desires set deep in our hearts seem like a luxury, granted only to those women who get their acts together. The message to the rest of us—whether from a driven culture or a driven church—is *try harder.*

Do you resonate with that? Do you ever feel that way? How have you—how are you now—"trying harder"?

The Heart of a Woman

And in all the exhortations we have missed the most important thing of all. We have missed the *heart* of a woman. And that is not a wise thing to do, for as the Scriptures tell us, the heart is central. "Above all else, guard your heart, for it is the wellspring of life" (Prov. 4:23 NKJV). Above all else.

Think about it: God created you as a woman. "God created man in his own image . . . male and female he created them" (Gen. 1:27 NKJV). Whatever it means to bear God's image, you do so as a woman. Female. That's how and where you bear his image. Your feminine heart has been created with the greatest of all possible dignities—as a reflection of God's own heart. You are a woman to your soul, to the very core of your being. And so the journey to discover what God meant when he created woman in his image—when he created you as his woman—that journey begins with your heart.

Is it a new thought to you that your heart as a woman is the most important thing about you? What does that mean to you?

To Be Romanced

Listen to your own heart and the hearts of the women you know. We think you'll find that every woman in her heart of hearts longs for three things: to be romanced, to play an irreplaceable role in a great adventure, and to unveil beauty. That's what makes a woman come alive.

Amen? Do you see those desires within your own heart? In the movies that you love? In your dreams? In your disappointments?

I will find you.
No matter how long it takes, no matter how far—I will find you.

—Nathaniel to Cora in *The Last of the Mohicans*

How do you think Cora felt as Nathaniel made this pledge to her?

The desire to be romanced is set deep in the heart of every little girl and every woman. By looking at the stories we love, we can get a hint, a clue to what those desires are. What were some of your favorite games as a little girl? Do you remember role-playing games that you played as a child? If you do, who or what did you like to pretend to be? A horse? A movie star? A mother? An undercover agent?

What were some of your favorite stories or movies while you were growing up?

What are some of your favorite stories and movies now?

Lifting the Veil

God is the Master Storyteller. He loves to use stories to capture our imaginations and speak to our hearts. There is a reason, a spiritual reason, why you love the stories you do. It would be good to ask God about that; to reveal the deeper reasons to you. It would be a good idea to make time in the next month or so to revisit them; rent the film, check out the book. Maybe make a "girls'night" and share some of your favorite movies with a friend.

Our guess is that although women also love adventure stories, heroic tales and battle epics, the stories that make your heart sigh with longing *most* are those that portray deeply meaningful relationships: specifically, good women being pursued, wanted, desired, and fought for by worthy, noble men. That desire is universal and written on the heart of every woman.

> When we are young, we want to be precious to someone—especially Daddy. As we grow older, the desire matures into a longing to be pursued, desired, wanted as a woman. Now, being romanced isn't all that a woman wants, and John and I are certainly not saying that a woman ought to derive the meaning of her existence from whether or not she is being or has been romanced by a man, but don't you see that you want this? To be desired, to be pursued by one who loves you, to be someone's priority? Most of our addictions as women flare up when we feel that we are not loved or sought after. At some core place, maybe deep within, perhaps hidden or buried in her heart, every woman wants to be seen, wanted, and pursued. We want to be romanced.

Do you want to be romanced? In what ways? (And if that desire seems far away, or undesirable, ask yourself, "Why is that? When did I lose that desire?")

An Irreplaceable Role in a Great Adventure

Sometime before the sorrows of life did their best to kill it in us, most young women wanted to be a part of something grand, something important. Before doubt and accusation take hold, most little girls sense that they have a vital role to play; they want to believe there is something in them that is needed and needed desperately.

Did you want to play a vital role in a great story?

I love remembering the story of the canoe trip on Oxbow Bend for many reasons, but chief among them is the fact that I was needed, and I did not fail. Are there places in your life where you feel that you are needed, vital, and essential? Do you like that?

What sort of adventures do you enjoy? And, do you enjoy them most by yourself or in sharing them with a close friend or loved one?

My guess is that although there are times when we need to be ALONE, for the most part, we want to share our lives, our experiences, our adventures, even our sorrows with others. As we wrote in *Captivating*, that is because,

> As echoes of the Trinity, we remember something. Made in the image of perfect relationship, we are relational to the core of our beings and filled with a desire for transcendent purpose. We long to be an irreplaceable part of a shared adventure.

Does that ring true to you? Do you want this?

Beauty to Unveil

What would it feel like to know that Jesus, your King, is enthralled by your beauty?

> *The King is enthralled by your beauty.*
>
> —Psalm 45:11 NIV

Little girls being raised in healthy homes have a sparkle in their eyes. They are like our little friend Lacey whose story we told of her flitting from office to office singing her newly made-up song. Most little girls enjoy playing dress up, wearing "twirl skirts." Did you? Take a moment and try to recall how you felt. What did you enjoy about it? If you have a young daughter, does she delight in playing "dress up"?

Do you remember a time when you were young that you wanted to be beautiful? When you wanted others to find you beautiful?

All little girls want to be delighted in. Their young hearts intuitively want to know they are lovely. Some will ask with words, "Am I lovely?" Others will simply ask with their eyes. Verbal or not, whether wearing a shimmery dress or covered in mud, all little girls want to know. When you were young, and your young heart asked the question "Am I lovely?" how were you answered?

By those whose opinions matter to you, how do you think you would be answered today?

The desire to be beautiful does not diminish with age. It remains. It is an ageless longing. Do you believe that?

Now, we know that the desire to be beautiful has caused many women untold grief (how many diets have you been on?). Countless tears have been shed and hearts broken in its pursuit. As Janis Ian sang, "I learned the truth at seventeen that love was meant for beauty queens, and high school girls with clear-skinned smiles." Beauty has been extolled and worshiped and kept just out of reach for most of us. For others, beauty has been shamed, used, and abused. Some of you have learned that possessing beauty can be dangerous. And yet—and this is just astounding—in spite of all the pain and distress that beauty has caused us as women, the desire remains.

How would you describe your feelings towards your own beauty? Ambivalent? Hopeless? Content? Longing?

Do you like having your picture taken? Do you like looking at those pictures later?

Lifting the Veil

Now this is key: The desire to be beautiful, to have a beauty all our own to unveil is not primarily about our looks. It is a desire to be captivating in the depths of who we are.

Who in your life is beautiful to you? Why?

Is it primarily because of their outward appearance, or is it more a matter of their heart?

This isn't about dresses and make-up. Beauty is so important that we'll come back to it again and again in this book. For now, don't you recognize that a woman yearns to be seen and to be thought of as captivating? We desire to possess a beauty that is worth pursuing, worth fighting for, a beauty that is core to who we truly are. *We want beauty that can be seen; beauty that can be felt; beauty that affects others; a beauty all our own to unveil.*

Do you want this beauty? Do you remember wanting it?

THE HEART OF A MAN

As I (John) described in *Wild at Heart*, there are three core desires in the heart of every man as well. (If you haven't read that book, you really should. It will open your eyes into the world of men.) But they are uniquely masculine. For starters, every man wants a battle to fight. It's the whole thing with boys and weapons. . . . Men also long for adventure. Boys love to climb and jump and see how fast they can ride their bikes (with no hands). Just look in your garage—all the gear and go-carts and motorcycles and ropes and boats and stuff. . . . Finally, every man longs for a beauty to rescue. They really do.

Have you seen that in the men you know? In your husband, brothers, friends and sons?

And, how have you felt about those desires in men? Do you like them? Encourage them?

Now—can you see how the desires of a man's heart and the desires of a woman's heart were at least *meant* to fit beautifully together? A woman in the presence of a good man, a real man, loves being a woman. His strength allows her feminine heart to flourish. His pursuit draws out her beauty. And a man in the presence of a real woman loves being a man. Her beauty arouses him to play the man, draws out his strength. She inspires him to be a hero. Would that we all were so fortunate.

As a woman, do you long to draw out the strength of a man?

By Way of the Heart

The longings God has written deep in your heart are telling you something essential about what it means to be a woman, and the life he meant for you to live. Now we know—many of those desires have gone unmet, or been assaulted, or simply so long neglected that most women end up living two lives. On the surface we are busy and efficient, professional, even. We are getting by. On the inside, women lose themselves in a fantasy world or in cheap novels, or we give ourselves over to food or some other addiction to numb the ache of our hearts. But your heart is still there, crying out to be set free, to find the life your desires tell you of.

You can find that life. If you are willing to embark on a great adventure. Are you aware of your heart wanting more?

Let's quiet our souls again and talk to God.

Dearest God. You fashioned my heart within. You knit me together in my mother's womb. You had your eye upon me before the foundation of the world. Would you please come again for me now and tenderly and firmly hold my heart? Awaken my desires. Restore them to me. Lead me into becoming the woman you created me to be; the woman I long to be. I will risk taking this journey with you . . . this journey into my heart, and into yours. I trust you. I love you. I need you. All this, and all the unspoken longings of my heart, I pray, in Jesus' name. Amen.

CHAPTER TWO

What Eve Alone Can Tell

Even to see her walk across the room is a liberal education.
—C. S. Lewis

Suddenly I turned around and she was standing there
With silver bracelets on her wrists and flowers in her hair
She walked up to me so gracefully and took my crown of thorns
Come in, she said I'll give you shelter from the storm.
—Bob Dylan

In the companion book this chapter begins by highlighting the progression of God's glorious creation. The creation story culminates with the creation of Eve. Eve is not an afterthought, not an appendage. Rather, she is the pinnacle, the crown of creation. The rest of the chapter is devoted to bringing into clarity the unique, essential, strong, and breathtaking ways that women bear the image of God. And it highlights that the core desires of a woman's heart are the very ways that she bears his image. They reflect God's core desires as well.

So dear heart, image-bearer of a beautiful God, take a deep breath and invite Jesus in.

Dear Jesus, I love you. I need you. I come before you now, once again, as yours, asking for your help, your grace. My life is yours. My heart is yours. Would you please come and shine your light into the depths of my heart that I might understand myself better and come to know your healing and your presence more deeply. Help me to remember what I need to remember. Help me to see, lift the veil of shame and help me to see what it means that I bear your own image—as a woman. Jesus, I give you access to all of my heart. I invite you into every part. Come, Holy Spirit, have your way—that I might love you, God, more deeply and truly with all of my heart, soul, mind, and strength. In Jesus' name I pray. Amen.

Windows to Your Heart

In this chapter we are exploring the wonder of Eve. What will help you imagine her? Think of the women you most admire, the women that have nearly taken your breath away because of their femininity. Are there characters in movies you'd like to see again? Or perhaps great works of art? (John mentioned "the stunning Greek sculpture of the goddess Nike of Samothrace, the winged beauty, just alighting on the prow of a great ship, her beautiful form revealed through the thin veils which sweep around her." You can view her at www.mlahanas.de/Greeks/Arts/Nike.htm.). To imagine Eve is not to compare ourselves to her, but rather to open up the possibility that we, too, are like her. We bear the image of God also.

At the same time, we are exploring the beauty of God. What helps you to appreciate his beauty? Is it music? Flowers? Some place in the outdoors? You might want to enjoy that again. And speaking of the Beauty of God, we love the song "Beautiful One," by By The Tree.

Now, look back over chapter two, skimming the pages. Did you highlight anything? What strikes you? What did it evoke in your heart?

What do you like about this chapter?

What do you not like about it? What are you struggling with?

What, if anything presented in this chapter are you having a hard time believing?

The Lost Princess

I was intrigued and enamored by Princess Anastasia. For a reason I could not explain, I felt a kinship with this mysterious princess, a connection to her—something deep in my heart whispered that I, too, was more than met the eye. Perhaps I, too, was a part of royalty, but my position had been lost. Perhaps I, too, was in disguise. My heart quickened at the thought of being a woman who was once a true princess. I don't think I'm alone in this. Have you ever wondered why the Cinderella story keeps haunting us? Not only is it a perennial favorite of little girls, women love it, too. Think of all the movies made along its themes, movies like *Pretty Woman* and *Ever After* and *A Cinderella Story* and *Maid in Manhattan.* Why is this notion of a hidden princess (and a prince who comes to find her) so enduring? Is there something in our hearts that is trying to speak to us? Is it just fantasy, escapism? Or is there something more?
Did you ever want to be Cinderella? Who have you dreamed of being?

The desire of a woman's heart and the realities of a woman's life seem an ocean apart. Oh, we long for romance and an irreplaceable role in a great story; we long for beauty. But that's not the life we have. The result is a sense of shame.

Is this true of you?

A woman's struggle with her sense of worth points to something glorious she was designed to be. The great emptiness we feel points to the great place we were created for.

Have you ever thought of your struggles and longings as pointing to something great you are designed to be?

Lifting the Veil

All those legends and fairy tales of the undiscovered Princess and the Beauty hidden as a maid are more accurate than we thought. There's a reason little girls resonate with them so. There is the classic *Cinderella* and *Ever After* and *Maid in Manhattan.* There is the animated version of *Anastasia,* as well as the old film version. There are universal themes here. Transcendent themes. Why not choose one this week and make time to watch it, alone or with a friend. Allow God to stir your heart and ask him to speak to you through the movies about who you are.

The Crown of Creation

Creation itself is a great work of art, and all works after it are echoes of the original. How it unfolded and where it reached its climax are mysteries worth unveiling. We will never truly understand women until we understand this.

What are some of your favorite works of art?

What are some of your favorite places of natural beauty?

Now, re-read the beginning of this chapter in the companion book that details the creation story. Do you see the progression? How would you describe it?

From water and stone, to pomegranate and rose, to leopard and nightingale, creation ascends in beauty. The plot is thickening; the symphony is building and swelling, higher and higher to a crescendo. No wonder "The morning stars sang together and all the angels shouted for joy" (Job 38:7 NKJV). A great hurrah goes up from the heavens. The greatest of all masterpieces is emerging. What was once formless and empty is now overflowing with life and color and sound and movement in a thousand variations. Most importantly, notice that each creature is more intricate and noble and mysterious than the last. A cricket is amazing, but it cannot compare to a wild horse.

Then something truly astonishing takes place. God sets his own image on the earth. He creates a being like himself. He creates a son.

> *The LORD God formed the man from the dust of the ground, and breathed into his nostrils the breath of life, and the man became a living being.*
>
> —GEN. 2:7 NKJV

It is worth noting here the glorious intimacy of man's creation. All the rest of God's masterpiece sprang into being merely from God speaking it to be. "Then God spoke . . ." But when it came time for God to create his image bearers, he *formed* them with his own hands. He breathed life into them himself.

What do you think about that?

It is nearing the end of the sixth day, the end of the Creator's great labor, as Adam steps forth, the image of God, the triumph of his work. He alone is pronounced the son of God. Nothing in creation even comes close. Picture Michelangelo's David. He is—magnificent. Truly the masterpiece seems complete. And yet, the Master says that something is not good, not right. Something is missing—and that something is Eve.

To make clear the point, what did God create last? Who is the final, astonishing work of God?

She is the crescendo, the final, astonishing work of God. Woman. In one last flourish creation comes to a finish not with Adam, but with *Eve.* She is the Master's finishing touch. How we wish this were an illustrated book, and we could show you now some painting or sculpture that captures this. Eve is—breathtaking.

Given the way creation unfolds, how it builds to ever higher and higher works of art, can there be any doubt that Eve is the crown of creation? Not an afterthought.

Not a nice addition like an ornament on a tree. She is God's final touch, his piéce de résistance. She fills a place in the world nothing and no one else can fill. Step to a window, ladies, if you can. Better still, find some place with a view. Look out across the earth and say to yourself, "The whole, vast world is incomplete without me. Creation reached its zenith in me."

How does that feel to you? Can you even do it? Ask God to reveal to you if this is true.

What Does Eve Speak to Us?

The story of Eve holds such rich treasures for us to discover. The essence and purpose of a woman is unveiled here in the story of her creation. These profound, eternal, mythic themes are written not just here in the coming of Eve, but in the soul of every woman after. Woman is the crown of creation—the most intricate, dazzling creature on earth. She has a crucial role to play, a destiny of her own.

And she, too, bears the image of God. But in a way that only the feminine can speak. What can we learn from her? God wanted to reveal something about himself, so he gave us Eve. When you are with a woman, ask yourself, *what is she telling me about God*? It will open up wonders for you.

Do this—ask yourself this very question. And . . . ?

Romance and Relationships: The Answer to Loneliness

Eve is created because things were not right without her. Something was not good. "It is not good for the man to be alone" (Gen. 2:18 NKJV). This just staggers us. Think of it. The world is young and completely unstained. Adam is yet in his innocence and full of glory. He walks with God. Nothing stands between them. They share something none of us has ever known—only longed for: an unbroken friendship, untouched by sin. Yet something is not good? Something is missing? What could it possibly be? Eve. Woman. Femininity. Wow. Talk about significance.

Have you thought about being a woman in this way? What would it do for your heart to embrace this truth?

> *Man's love is of man's life a thing*
> *apart*
> *'Tis a woman's whole existence.*
>
> —Byron

To be specific, what was "not good" was the fact that the man was "alone." "It is not good for the human to be alone; I shall make him a sustainer beside him." How true this is. Whatever else we know about women, we know they are relational creatures to their core. While little boys are killing one another in mock battles on the playground, little girls are negotiating relationships. If you want to know how people are doing, what's going on in our world, don't ask me—ask Stasi. I don't call friends and chat with them on the phone for an hour. I can't tell you who's dating whom, who's feelings have been hurt—ask Stasi. This is so second nature, so assumed among women that it goes unnoticed by them.

What have you been thinking about lately? What occupies most of your concerns? Are they relationships, people, loved ones?

Most women *define* themselves in terms of their relationships, and the quality they deem those relationships to have. I am a mother, a sister, a daughter, a friend. Or, I am alone. I'm not seeing anyone right now, or my children aren't calling, or my friends seem distant. This is not a weakness in women—it is a glory. A glory that reflects the heart of God.

How *do* you define yourself? If you were to introduce yourself, what would you say?

God's Heart for Relationship

The vast desire and capacity a woman has for intimate relationships tells us of God's vast desire and capacity for intimate relationships. In fact, this may be the most important thing we ever learn about God—that he yearns for relationship with us. "Now this is eternal life: that they may know you, the only true God" (John 17:3 NKJV). The whole story of the Bible is a love story between God and his people. He yearns for us. He cares. He has a tender heart.

Have you seen God as yearning for you? As longing to be loved *by you*?

Lifting the Veil

After years of hearing the heart-cry of women, I am convinced beyond a doubt of this: God wants to be loved. He wants to be a priority to someone. How could we have missed this? From cover to cover, from beginning to end, the cry of God's heart is, "Why won't you choose me?" It is amazing to me how humble, how vulnerable God is on this point. "You will find me," says the Lord, "when you seek me with all of your heart" (Jer. 29:13 NKJV). In other words, "Look for me, pursue me—I want you to pursue me." Amazing. As Tozer says, "God waits to be wanted."

What does God want? (Mark 12:29–30; Matt. 22:36–38)

Do you want this, too?

Life changes dramatically when romance comes into our lives. Christianity changes dramatically when we discover that it, too, is a great romance. That God yearns to share a life of beauty, intimacy, and adventure with us. "I have loved you with an everlasting love" (Jer. 31:3 NKJV). This whole world was made for romance—the rivers and the glens, the meadows and beaches. Flowers, music, a kiss. But we have a way of forgetting all that, losing ourselves in work and worry. Eve—God's message to the world in feminine form—invites us to romance. Through her God makes romance a priority of the universe.

I think most women are a little embarrassed by their deep longings to be romanced. Are you? Is this something you openly share with others?

How does it change the way you feel about your own heart's desires to hear that through Eve God makes romance a priority of the universe?

So God endows Woman with certain qualities which are essential to relationship, qualities that speak of God. She is inviting. She is vulnerable. She is tender. She embodies mercy. She is also fierce and fiercely devoted. As the old saying goes, "Hell hath no fury like a woman scorned." That's just how God acts when he isn't chosen. "I, the LORD your God, am a jealous God who will not share your affection with any other god!" (Ex. 20:5 NLT). A woman's righteous jealousy speaks of the jealousy of God for us. Tender and inviting, intimate and alluring, fiercely devoted. O yes, our God has a passionate, romantic heart. Just look at Eve.

How are you doing on these qualities these days? How have you been—or perhaps not been . . .

Inviting?

Vulnerable?

Tender?

Merciful?

Fiercely devoted?

Jealous?(!)

God creates Eve to keep relationship at the center of life. It's central to a woman's design—and her reason for being. Do you feel like you've been keeping relationship a high priority? What would you want to do to make it more central to your life—and the lives of those you love?

An Adventure to Share

While Eve has a glory for relationship, that is *not* all she is essential for. Back in Genesis, when God sets his image bearers on the earth, he gives them their mission:

> And God said, "Let us make a human in our image, by our likeness, to hold sway over the fish of the sea and the fowl of the heavens and the cattle and the wild beasts and all the crawling things that crawl upon the earth.
>
> And God created the human in his image,
> in the image of God He created him,
> male and female He created them.
>
> And God blessed them, and God said to them, "Be fruitful and multiply and fill the earth and conquer it, and hold sway over the fish of the sea and the fowl of the heavens and every beast that crawls upon the earth."—Gen. 1:26–28 (PARAPHRASED)

Call it the Human Mission—to be all and do all God sent us here to do. And notice: the mission to be fruitful and conquer and hold sway is given *both* to Adam *and* to Eve. "And God said to *them* . . ." (Gen.1:28). Eve is standing right there when God gives the world over to us. She has a vital role to play; she is a partner in this great adventure. All that human beings were intended to do here on earth—all the creativity and exploration, all the battle and rescue and nurture—we were intended to do *together.* In fact, not only is Eve needed, she is *desperately* needed.

Is this a new thought to you? How does it make you feel?

When God creates Eve, he calls her an *ezer kenegdo.* "It is not good for the man to be alone, I shall make him a [*ezer kenegdo*]" (Gen. 2:18 NKJV). Hebrew scholar Robert Alter, who has spent years translating the book of Genesis, says that this phrase is "notoriously difficult to translate." The various attempts we have in English are "helper" or "companion" or the notorious "help meet." Why are these translations so incredibly wimpy, boring, flat, and disappointing? What is a help meet, anyway? What little girl dances through the house singing "One day I shall be a help meet?" Helper? Sounds like *Hamburger Helper.*

What have you thought a "Help Meet" was? Is it something you aspired to become? Dreamed of?

The translations have been flat. I personally thought that being a help meet meant that men had the important lives and women's big job was to help them have it. I was second place and second best. I didn't much like being created as an unimportant, afterthought *helper.* I didn't like being an *ezer kenegdo,* but that's because I didn't truly understand what it was!

Alter is getting close when he translates it "sustainer beside him." The word *ezer* is used only 20 other places in the entire Old Testament. And in every other instance the person being described is God himself, when you *desperately* need him to come through for you.

> *There is no one like the God of Jeshurun, who rides on the heavens to help you . . . Blessed are you, O Israel! Who is like you, a people saved by the* Lord*? He is your shield and helper and your glorious sword.*
>
> —Deuteronomy 33:26, 29 NKJV

> *I lift up my eyes to the hills—where does my help come from? My help comes from the* Lord*, the Maker of heaven and earth.*
>
> —Psalm 121:1–2 NKJV

Most of the contexts are life and death, by the way, and God is your only hope. Your *ezer*. If he is not there beside you, you are dead. A better translation, therefore, of *ezer* would be "life-saver." *Kenegdo* means alongside, or opposite to, a counterpart. You see, the life God calls us to is not a safe life. Ask Joseph, Abraham, Moses, Deborah, Esther—any of the friends of God from the Old Testament. Ask Mary and Lazarus, ask Peter, James and John, ask Priscilla and Aquila—any of the friends of God in the New Testament. God calls us to a life involving frequent risks and many dangers. Why else would we need him to be our *ezer*? You don't need a life-saver if your mission is to be a couch potato. You need an *ezer* when your life is in constant danger.

Like Arwen, in the mythic trilogy, *The Lord of the Rings*, you are an *ezer*. A life-saver. Let that be true. How does it change the way you look at yourself?

Does it elevate the role of woman?

That longing in the heart of a woman to share life together as a great adventure—that comes straight from the heart of God, who also longs for this. He does not want to be an option in our lives. He does not want to be an appendage, a tag-along. Neither does any woman. God is essential. He wants us to need him—desperately. Eve is essential. She has an irreplaceable role to play. And so you'll see that women are endowed with fierce devotion, an ability to suffer great hardships, a vision to make the world a better place.

How does your heart respond?

Beauty to Unveil

That we even need to explain how beauty is so *absolutely essential* to God only shows how dull we have grown to him, to the world in which we live, and to Eve. Beauty is essential to God. No—that's not putting it strongly enough. Beauty is the essence of God. The first way we know this is through nature, the world God has given us. Scripture says that the created world is filled with the glory of God (Is. 6:3). In what way? Primarily through its *beauty*. The earth in summer is brimming with beauty, beauty of such magnificence and variety and unembarrassed lavishness, ripe beauty, lush beauty, beauty given to us with such generosity and abundance it is almost scandalous.

Nature is not primarily functional. It is primarily beautiful. Stop for a moment and let that sink in. We're so used to evaluating everything (and everyone) by their usefulness, this thought will take a minute or two to begin to dawn on us. Nature is not primarily functional. It is primarily *beautiful*. Which is to say, beauty is in and of itself a great and glorious good, something we need in large and daily doses (for our God has seen fit to arrange for this). Nature at the height of its glory shouts *Beauty is Essential!* revealing that Beauty is the essence of God.

What does this stir in you?

Write down some of your favorite places to visit, the places in nature and in the world that take your breath away. Why do you love to go there?

WHY BEAUTY MATTERS

Beauty is powerful. It may be the most powerful thing on earth. It is dangerous. Because it *matters.*

Does beauty matter to you? In your home? In your appearance? In others?

> *Every experience of beauty points to [eternity].*
>
> —HANS URS VON BALTHASAR

Lifting the Veil

Beauty is such a source of struggle for women. So let's really dig deep here—for clarity, and for the healing of our hearts. Beauty matters to God. Very much. But lest you fall into despair, here is very good news. You possess it. Yes, you. True beauty. (I know you just rolled your eyes, by the way.) It may take the whole book to begin to clear this up, so hang in there. Let the emotions come. Invite Jesus into the whole way you feel about beauty—especially your beauty.

Beauty is powerful. It is dangerous. It matters. Let's explore why.

First, beauty *speaks.*

And what does beauty say to us? Think of what it is like to be caught in traffic for over an hour: Horns blaring, people shouting obscenities. Exhaust pouring in your windows, suffocating you. Then remember what it's like to come into a beautiful place, a garden or a meadow or a quiet beach. There is room for your soul. It expands. You can breathe again. You can rest. It is good. All is well. I sit outside on a summer evening and just listen and behold and drink it all in, and my heart begins to quiet, and peace begins to come into my soul. My heart tells me that "All will be well," as Julian of Norwich concluded: "And all manner of things will be well." That is what beauty says: *All shall be well.*

What does your heart feel when you come into a spacious, lovely place?

Being with a woman who is at rest, a woman comfortable within her own beauty, is an enjoyable experience. She is trusting God, not *striving to become* beautiful, but allowing his beauty to more fully inhabit her. Have you had the experience of being with a woman who was stressed, striving, worried? And how did you feel around her?

Have you had the pleasure of being with a woman who is resting in God and knowing that all will be well? How did you feel around her?

Which kind of woman do you tend to be?

BEAUTY ALSO *INVITES.*

Recall what it is like to hear a truly beautiful piece of music. It captures you; you want to sit down and just drink it in. We buy the CD and play it many times over. (This is not visual, showing us that beauty is deeper than looks.) Music like this commands your attention, invites you to come more deeply into it.

What music are you listening to these days that does this for your soul?

The same is true of a beautiful garden, or a scene in nature. You want to enter in, explore, partake of it, feast upon it. We describe a great book as "captivating." It draws you in, holds your attention. You can't wait to get back to it, spend time with it. All of the responses that God wants of us. All of the responses a woman wants, too.

Would the friends who know you well describe you as an inviting woman? Why did you answer the way you did?

Beauty *nourishes.* It is a kind of food our souls crave. A woman's breast is among the loveliest of all God's works, and it is with her breast she nourishes a baby—a stunning picture of the way in which Beauty itself nourishes us. In fact, a woman's body is one of the most beautiful of all God's creations. "Too much of eternity," as Blake said, "for the eye of man." It nourishes, offers life. That is such a profound metaphor for Beauty itself. As Lewis said,

We do not want merely to see beauty, though, God knows, even that is bounty enough. We want something else which can hardly be put into words—to be united with the beauty we see, to pass into it, to receive it into ourselves *(The Weight of Glory).*

Have you had that experience? Where? When? What was it like?

Beauty *comforts.* There is something profoundly healing about it. Have you ever wondered why we send flowers to the bereaved? In the midst of their suffering and loss, only a gift of beauty says enough, or says it right. After I lost my dearest friend Brent, there were months where only beauty helped. I could not hear words of counsel. I could not read or even pray. Only beauty helped.

How have you been comforted by beauty?

Beauty *inspires.* After beholding all the marvelous wonders of the creation of Narnia (as told in *The Magician's Nephew* by C.S. Lewis), the cabbie says, "Glory be! I'd have been a better man all my life if I'd known there were things like this!" Or as Jack Nicholson says to Helen Hunt at the end of *As Good as It Gets,* "You make me want to be a better man." Isn't it true? Think of what it might have been like to have been in the presence of a woman like Mother Teresa. Her life was so beautiful, and it called us to something higher. A teacher in the inner city explained to us why he insisted on putting a fountain and flowers in the courtyard of the building. "Because these children need to be inspired. They need to know that life can be better." Beauty inspires.

Think of the women that inspire you: what is it about their lives that calls you to something more?

Beauty is *transcendent.* It is our most immediate experience of the eternal. Think of what it's like to behold a gorgeous sunset, or the ocean at dawn. Remember the ending of a great story. We yearn to linger, to experience it all our days. Sometimes the beauty is so deep it pierces us with longing. For what? For life as it was meant to be. Beauty reminds us of an Eden we have never known, but somehow know our hearts were created for. Beauty speaks of heaven to come, when all shall be beautiful. It haunts us with eternity. Beauty says, *There is a glory calling to you.* And if there is a glory, there is a source of glory. What great goodness could have possibly created this? What generosity gave us this to behold? Beauty draws us to God.

When has an experience of beauty pierced you with longing? Can you describe it?

All these things are true for any experience of Beauty. But they are *especially* true when we experience the beauty of a woman—her eyes, her form, her voice, her heart, her spirit, her life. She speaks all of this far more profoundly than anything else in all creation, because she is *incarnate,* she is personal. It flows to us from an immortal being. She is beauty through and through. "For where is any author in the world/ Teaches such beauty as a woman's eye?" (Shakespeare). Beauty is, without question, the most *essential* and the most *misunderstood* of all of God's qualities—of all feminine qualities, too. We know it has caused untold pain in the lives of women. But even there something is speaking. Why so much heartache over beauty? We don't ache over being geniuses or fabulous hockey players. Women ache over the issue of beauty—they ache to be beautiful, to believe they are beautiful, and they worry over keeping it if ever they can find it.

Okay—let your heart speak about the ache. What does this whole subject of beauty stir in you, in the way of an ache? And why?

But Why a Beauty to *Unveil?*

One of the deepest ways a woman bears the image of God is in her mystery. By mystery we don't mean "forever beyond your knowing," but "something to be explored." "It is the glory of God to conceal a matter," says the book of Proverbs, "to search out a matter is the glory of kings" (25:2 NKJV). God yearns to be known, but he wants to be *sought after* by those who would know him. He says, "You shall find me when you seek me with all your heart" (Jer. 29:13 NKJV).

Are you aware of this yearning, as a woman? And *are* you being sought after these days?

Whatever else it means to be feminine, it is depth and mystery and complexity, with beauty as their very essence. Now, lest despair set in, let us say as clearly as we can:

Every woman has a beauty to unveil.

Every woman.

Because she bears the image of God. She doesn't have to conjure it, go get it from a salon, have plastic surgery or a breast implant. No, beauty is an *essence* that is given to every woman at her creation.

What if? What if this really *is* true about you—that you *are* a captivating woman? Let your heart go there for a moment; what does it bring?

Lifting the Veil

Beauty is the essence of femininity. Not the only essence, but very much core to who and what a woman is. It was given to every woman at her birth, in her creation as an image-bearer of a captivating God. Now, we know that life has assaulted your heart and your beauty, and because of that, most women doubt very much that they are beautiful. We'll say much more about that in a minute. But let your heart rest for now in this: God is beautiful. He has given you his very image, deep in your soul. That means you have a beauty to unveil, too.

O Jesus, come into this place in my heart. Help me to believe that you have given me your beauty. That I am a woman through and through, and because of your creation in me, I, too, have a heart for romance, I, too, am a life-saver, and I do have beauty to offer the world. I ask this in your name. Amen.

CHAPTER THREE

Haunted by a Question

She knew treachery,
Rapine, deceit and lust, and ills enow
To be a woman.
—JOHN DONNE

O most pernicious woman!
—WILLIAM SHAKESPEARE

The fall of Eve is felt every day of our lives. We experience it at the hands of other women, and we grieve it in our own souls. We live a life marred by fallenness; things break, laundry never ends, monotony weighs us down, and on any given day sin rises up out of our flesh when we least expect it. We respond with quick anger. We don't tell the whole truth. Once again we are exposed as not being all that we were made to be, all that we long to be.

The grocery store story at the beginning of the companion chapter is meant to highlight the fact that our fallenness reveals itself in the every-day matters of life. How we drive. What we say. What we don't say. How we experience others. What we buy. How we react when someone cuts us off on the highway.

Before we go any further, however, let us turn the gaze of our souls to our God. He knows us. He sees it all. And he returns our gaze with a heart full of love and with mercy in his eyes.

Dear Jesus, I love you. I need you. I come before you now, once again, as yours, asking for your help, your grace. My life is yours. My heart is yours. Would you please come and shine your light into the depths of my heart that I might understand myself better and come to know your healing and your presence more deeply? Help me to remember what I need to remember. Help me to see, to understand, to repent, to forgive and to become. Jesus, I give you access to all of my heart. I invite you into every part. Come, Holy Spirit, have your way . . . that I might love you, God, more deeply and truly with all of my heart, soul, mind, and strength. In Jesus' name I pray. Amen.

Windows to Your Soul

We talk about two basic ways in which women are fallen: either they become dominating and controlling, or desolate and clingy. Can you name a few characters from movies that fit either description? How about the women in *Steel Magnolias*? *Fried Green Tomatoes*? *Sense and Sensibility*? *Forrest Gump*?

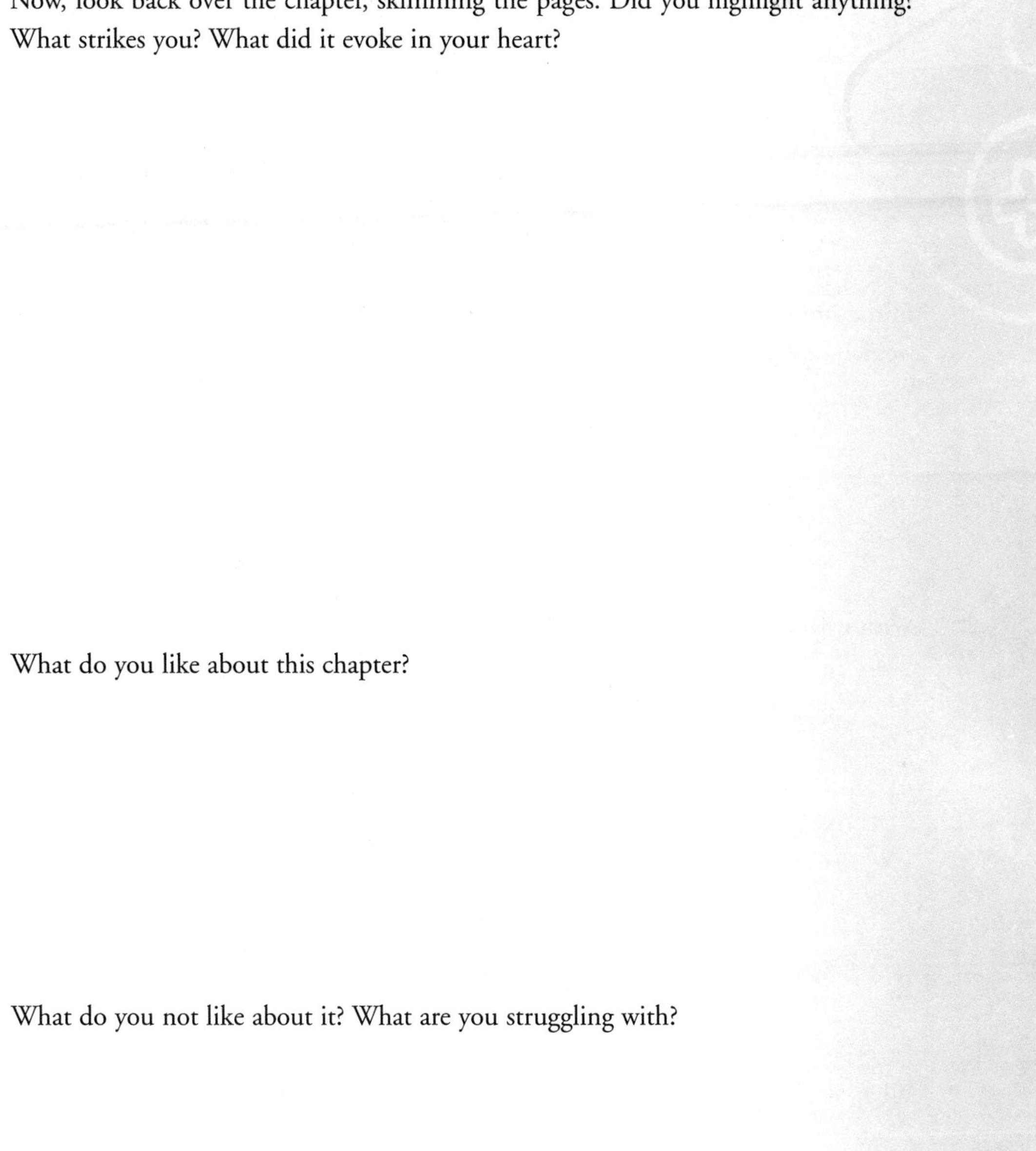

Now, look back over the chapter, skimming the pages. Did you highlight anything? What strikes you? What did it evoke in your heart?

What do you like about this chapter?

What do you not like about it? What are you struggling with?

How does your fallen nature most often reveal itself?

In the broad categories, would you say you lean more towards being a controlling woman or a desolate woman?

With what do you tend to indulge your heart?

What, if anything, presented in this chapter are you having a hard time believing?

What's Happened to Us?

Eve was given to the world as the incarnation of a beautiful, captivating God—a life-offering, life-saving lover, a relational specialist, full of tender mercy and hope. Yes, she brought a strength to the world, but not a striving, sharp-edged strength. She was inviting, alluring, captivating.

Is that how you experience the women you know? Is that how people experience you?

Why do so few women have anything close to a life of romance? Loneliness and emptiness are far more common themes—so entirely common that most women buried their longings for romance long ago and are living now merely to survive, get through the week. And it's not just romance—why are most of the relationships of women fraught with hardship? Their friendships, their families, their best friends all seem to have come down with a sort of virus that makes them fundamentally unavailable, leaving a woman lonely at the end of the day. Even when relationships are good, it's never enough.

Are you aware of loneliness deep within your heart?

And women are tired. We are drained. But it's not from a life of shared adventures. No, the weariness of women comes from lives that are crammed with routine, with chores, with hundreds of demands. Somehow, somewhere between our youth and yesterday, *efficiency* has taken the place of adventure. Most women do not feel they are playing an irreplaceable role in a great Story. O no. We struggle to know if we matter at all. If we are at home, we feel ashamed we don't have a "real life" in the outside world. We are swallowed by laundry. If we have a career, we feel as though we are missing out on more important matters like marriage and children. We are swallowed by meetings.

At some level, do you feel like a hamster on a wheel—running, running? Are you busy? Are you tired?

A Woman's Deepest Question

Finally, most women doubt very much that they have any genuine beauty to unveil. It is, in fact, our deepest doubt. When it comes to the issues surrounding beauty, we vacillate between striving and resignation. New diets, new outfits, new hair color. Work out, work on your life, try this discipline or that new program for self-improvement. Oh, forget it. Who cares anyway? Put up a shield and get on with life. Hide. Hide in busyness, hide in church activities, hide in depression. There is nothing captivating about me. Certainly not *inside* of me. I'll be lucky to pull it off on the outside.

When I'm going out to a party or gathering, or just to dinner at a friend's house—really, anywhere I am meeting other people—I feel nervous. Often, I'm not aware of what I'm truly feeling, but I find myself reapplying lipstick in the car on the way. The more nervous I feel, the more lipstick goes on. Getting close to the destination, I reapply more lipstick. A little closer, on goes some more. Turning into their street, on goes another layer of Sunset Rose or whatever. I clued into this "habit" some time ago when I caught myself putting on another unnecessary layer. What was I doing? *I was afraid.* At least if my makeup looks good, something deep inside me reasoned, maybe I won't be exposed. Found out. Seen.

Can you relate to my lipstick story? Are you aware of the ways in which you hide, trying not to be "seen"?

Every woman in the core of her being is haunted by Eve. She knows, if only when she passes a mirror, that she is not what she was meant to be. We are more keenly aware of our own shortcomings than anyone else. Remembering the glory that was once ours awakens my heart to an ache that has long gone unfulfilled. It's almost too much to hope for, too much to have lost.

Are you aware of your own beauty? (You possess it, dear one. You do.) How did you feel exploring Eve in the last chapter?

Little girls want to know, *Am I lovely?* The twirling skirts, the dress-up, the longing to be pretty and to be seen—that is what that's all about. We are seeking an answer to our Question. When I was a girl of maybe five years old, I remember standing on top of the coffee table in my grandparents' living room and singing my heart out. I wanted to capture attention, especially my father's attention. I wanted to be captivating. We all did. But for most of us, the answer to our Question when we were young was "No. There is nothing captivating about you. Get off the coffee table." Nearly all a woman does now is fueled by her longing to be delighted in, her longing to be beautiful, to be irreplaceable, to have her Question answered "Yes!"

Is that the first time you've heard that core Question, "Am I lovely?" put into words? Are you aware that it *is* a woman's core question?

The Fall of Eve

Lifting the Veil

As we enter into an honest look at how we—like Eve—are not what we were meant to be, that we, too, have fallen, we do so under the banner of God's love.

His banner over me is love (Song 2:4 NKJV).

We do so knowing that we are under no condemnation—Jesus has taken care of our every sin.

There is now no condemnation for those who are in Christ Jesus (Rom. 8:1 NKJV).

Most women go to shame and self-contempt so quickly. It's a way of hiding, a way of not really dealing with our lives. But we live under total grace and complete forgiveness, and because that is true, we can look at the ways we control and cling and demand and hide so that we might forsake all that for our freedom in Christ and live a true life.

When the world was young and we were innocent—both man and woman—we were "naked and unashamed" (Gen. 2:25 NKJV). Nothing to hide. Simply . . . glorious. And while that world was young and we, too, were young and beautiful and full of life, a corner was turned. Something happened which we have heard about but never fully understood.

We fell.

The woman was convinced. The fruit looked so fresh and delicious, and it would make her so wise! So she ate some of the fruit. She also gave some to her husband, who was with her. Then he ate it, too (Gen. 3:6 NLT).

The woman was convinced. Convinced of what?

She was convinced that God was holding out on her. Convinced she could not trust his heart toward her. In order to have the life she believed she needed, she was convinced she must take matters into her own hands. And so she did.

Look into your own heart. Ask God to gently show you where you have this tendency as well.

Eve failed as Adam's *ezer kenegdo.* Rather than bringing him life, she invited him to his death. And Adam failed Eve as well. He offered not his strength but his silence; not his protection but his passivity.

Have you seen this played out in your life? Seen it this week? Last night?

The Curse

To the woman he said,

> *"I will greatly increase your pains in childbearing;*
> *with pain you will give birth to children.*
> *Your desire will be for your husband,*
> *and he will rule over you."*

To Adam he said,

> *"Because you listened to your wife and ate from*
> *the tree about which I commanded you,*
> *'You must not eat of it,'*
> *"Cursed is the ground because of you;*
> *through painful toil you will eat of it*
> *all the days of your life.*
> *It will produce thorns and thistles for you. . . ."*
>
> —Genesis 3:16–18 NKJV

Now, it would be good for us to give careful attention to all that has unfolded here, especially the curses God pronounced, for the story explains our lives today, east of Eden. For one thing, the curse on Adam cannot be limited only to actual thorns and thistles. If that were so, then every man who chooses not to be a farmer gets to escape the curse. Take a white-collar job, and you're Scot-free. No, the meaning is deeper, and the implications are for every son of Adam. Man is cursed with futility and failure. Life is going to be hard for a man now, in the place he will feel it most. Failure is a man's worst fear.

In just the same way, the curse for Eve and all her daughters cannot be limited only to babies and marriage, for if that were true then every single woman without children gets to escape the curse. Not so. The meaning is deeper, and the implications are for every daughter of Eve. Woman is cursed with loneliness (relational heartache), with the urge to control (especially her man), and with the dominance of men (which is not how things were meant to be, and we are not saying it is a good thing—it is the fruit of the Fall and a sad fact of history). I am also indebted to Dan Allender, who first pointed out these insights to me.

What are your deepest heartaches? Your deepest worries?

Do you see the relational aspects of your sorrow?

Are you aware of an emotional ache? An emptiness?

Did you think it was just you? Something fundamentally and uniquely wrong with you?

Lifting the Veil

OK. Now it's time to look "in the closet." None of us are off the hook here. Jesus has redeemed us, and we are in the process of becoming all he intended (sanctified). But, sadly, we still manifest the fallen nature. However, when we see it, we can identify it, and repent of it. Don't be afraid. You're not alone here.

When a man goes bad, as every man has in some way gone bad after the Fall, what is most deeply marred is his strength. He either becomes a passive, weak man—strength surrendered—or he becomes a violent, driven man—strength unglued. When a woman falls from grace, what is most deeply marred is her tender vulnerability, beauty that invites to life. She becomes a dominating, controlling woman, a desolate, needy, mousy woman, or some odd combination of both, depending on her circumstances.

Dominating Women

Think for a moment about the characters of women you dislike, even despise, in movies. (That seems a more charitable place to start—they are, after all, fictional characters). In *The Horse Whisperer*, Annie MacLean (played by Kristin Scott Thomas) is a sharp, sophisticated New York professional, and the editor of a leading women's magazine. She is also an incredibly controlling woman. Her daughter is hospitalized in critical condition following the accident which takes the life of her best friend, claims her leg, and terribly injures her horse. Understandably, Annie is shaken to the core. How she handles her crisis is to dominate—the doctors, the nurses, her husband, even her maimed daughter. At one point she notices her daughter's IV bag is running low:

> "You can't leave it to these people."
> (She steps into the hall, apprehends the first nurse coming by.)
> "Excuse me—my daughter needs a new IV."
> "Yes, I know—we have her down . . ."
> "Well I'd like you to take care of it now please."
> ("Please" is a barely veiled threat, more like, "or else.") Annie walks back into

the room and explains to her embarrassed husband:
"You have to stay on top of these people constantly."

She needs no one. She is in charge—"on top of things constantly." She is a woman who knows how to get what she wants. (Some of us might even admire that!) But consider this—there is nothing merciful about her, nothing tender, and certainly nothing vulnerable. She has forsaken essential aspects of her femininity.

Annie offers a good picture of the dominating, controlling woman. I imagine that in her presence, one would feel immense pressure to come through, buck up, *perform.* What would it feel like to be the daughter of a dominating, controlling woman? What would it feel like to be her friend?

Fallen Eve controls her relationships. She refuses to be vulnerable. And if she cannot secure her relationships, then she kills her heart's longing for intimacy so that she will be safe and in control. She becomes a woman "who doesn't need anyone—especially a man." How this plays out over the course of her life, and how the wounds of her childhood shape her heart's convictions are often a complex story, one worth knowing. But beneath it all, behind it all, is a simple truth: Women dominate and control because they fear their vulnerability. Far from God and far from Eden, it seems a perfectly reasonable way to live.

Controlling women are those of us who don't trust anyone else to drive our car. Or help in our kitchen. Or speak at our retreat or our meeting. Or carry something for us. Make a decision that is "ours" to make. Suggest a different dress, agenda, restaurant, route. We room alone when we travel. We plan perfect birthday parties for our children. It might look like we're simply "trying to be a good mom" or a good friend, but what we often do is arrange other people's lives. Controlling women are "the sort of women," as C.S. Lewis said, "Who 'live for others.' You can tell the others by their hunted expression."

Ugh. I know this to be true. I see it in myself. I tend to "go to control" when my life feels chaotic. If my boys are getting too loud, too rambunctious, too demanding, I clamp down. I start giving orders, barking out my demands for behavioral changes. It never brings my desired results of a peaceful home. In what ways are you a controlling, dominating woman?

Would your children, your husband, or your friends and coworkers say you are controlling?

Controlling women tend to be very well rewarded in this fallen world of ours. We are the ones to receive corporate promotions. We are the ones put in charge of our women's ministries. "Can do, Bottom Line, Get-It-Done" kinds of women.

In what ways have *you* been rewarded for being this kind of woman?

Do you like being vulnerable? Are you comfortable trusting your well-being to someone else?

Do you see that this self-protective strategy of behavior stems from fear? Does that help you have more mercy for yourself? For others?

Lifting the Veil

Women can be strong in very holy ways. Read the story of Rahab (Exodus 2) or the story of Deborah (Judges 4). We are not saying that strength in a woman is wrong. Not at all. However, thanks to the Fall, far too many women use their strength in self-protective ways, ways that violate love, tenderness, and mercy. They forfeit their femininity in order to feel safe and in control. Choosing to live in a dominating, controlling way causes something precious in us to be lost. Something the world needs very much.

Desolate Women

If on the one side of the spectrum we find that Fallen Eve becomes hard, rigid, and controlling, then on the other side you find women who are desolate, needy, far *too* vulnerable. Women like Kathy Bates' character at the beginning of *Fried Green Tomatoes.* She is naive, lost, bereft of any sense of self. She falls under the abuse of a bad man and hasn't the will to get herself out. Take out the abusive situations, and you have a woman like Marianne in *Sense and Sensibility*, who is far too willing to give herself over to an untrustworthy man. She is desperate to be loved. And she ends up heartbroken.

Desolate women are ruled by the aching abyss within them. These are the women who buy books like *Men Who Hate Women and the Women Who Love Them* and *Women Who Love Too Much* and *Co-dependent No More*. They are consumed by a hunger for relationship.

Are there people in your life that you would describe as desolate? In what ways?

Are there times when this would describe you? In what ways?

What would it feel like to be the daughter of a desolate, needy, mousy woman? What would it feel like to be her friend?

What is there about *you* that you would like to keep hidden from the eyes of those around you?

If they saw what you are trying to hide, what are you afraid their response would be?

Lifting the Veil

What would it be like to ask those you love and live with, what you are like to live with? Or to ask your friends, how they experience you as a woman? Too risky? Pray about it. It can be a very scary thing to do but also a very enlightening thing as well.

Like Eve after she tasted the forbidden fruit, we women hide. We hide behind our make up. We hide behind our humor. We hide with angry silences and punishing withdrawals. We hide our truest selves and offer only what we believe is wanted, what is safe. Hiding women are those of us who never speak up at a Bible study or PTA counsel or any kind of meeting. Who, when we pass a beautiful dress in a window, say to ourselves, *I could never wear that.* We stay busy at family gatherings and parties we can't avoid. We'd rather go to a movie than out to dinner with a friend. We don't initiate sex with our husbands—ever. We dismiss every compliment. We relinquish major decisions to others.

What in that description have you done? How do you hide?

Lifting the Veil

Sometimes it is hard to admit our fallen ways. We know many women who defend their style of controlling or hiding. They see it as "necessary" or "not a big deal or "just my personality." Far from God and far from Eden, it seems a perfectly reasonable way to live.

But that is not entirely true.

Consider also this: "Whatever is not from faith is sin" (Rom. 14:23). That self-protective way of relating to others has nothing to do with real loving and nothing to do with deeply trusting God. It is our gut-level response to a dangerous world. We take matters into our own hands. We don't return to our God with our broken and desperate hearts.

And it has never occurred to us that in all our controlling and hiding something precious is also lost—something the world needs from us so very, very much.

INDULGING

Whether we tend to dominate and control, or withdraw in our desolation and hide, still . . . the ache remains. The deep longings in our heart as a woman just won't go away. And so we indulge.

We buy ourselves something nice when we aren't feeling appreciated. We "allow" ourselves a second helping of ice cream or a Super-Sized something when we are lonely. We move into a fantasy world to find some water for our thirsty hearts. Romance novels (a billion-dollar industry), soap operas, talk shows, gossip, the myriads of women's magazines all feed an inner life of relational dreaming and voyeurism that substitutes—for awhile—for the real thing. But none of these really satisfy, and so we find ourselves trying to fill the remaining emptiness with our little indulgences (we call them "bad habits"). Brent Curtis calls them our "little affairs of the heart."

Does this need more explanation? I don't think so. Indulging is a less subtle form of taking matters into our own hands. Or as my friend Leigh says, trying to suck life off of the end of a fork. But we certainly don't limit our indulging to eating. What are some ways you indulge your heart? Where do you go instead of to God when the ache of your heart begins to make itself known? What from the above list is true of you? What else would you add?

We need not be ashamed that our hearts ache, that we need and thirst and hunger for much more. All of our hearts ache. All of our hearts are at some level unsatisfied and longing. It is our insatiable need for more that drives us to our God. What we need to see is that all our controlling and our hiding, all our indulging, actually serves to separate us from our hearts. We lose touch with those longings that make us a woman. And they never, ever resolve the deeper issue of our souls.

Have your indulgences brought a lasting comfort, intimacy, and sense of being alive as a woman?

Eve's Lingering Fear

Every woman knows now that she is not what she was meant to be. And she fears that soon it will be known—if it hasn't already been discovered—and that she will be abandoned. Left alone to die a death of the heart. That is a woman's worst fear—abandonment.

Take a moment. Underneath, in the deepest recesses of your heart . . . is this fear there? The fear that you will end up abandoned and alone?

Take a moment and invite God in. Into the places in your heart where you feel you need to hide or control or indulge in order to be safe and well. Ask him to speak to you about these places . . . and to give you the courage to begin to trust him with your life in ever deeper ways.

And down in the depths of our hearts, our Question remains. Unanswered. Or rather, it remains answered in the way it was answered so badly in our youth: "Am I lovely? Do you see me? Do you want to see? Are you captivated by what you find in me?" We live haunted by that Question yet unaware that it still needs an answer.

When we were young, we knew nothing about Eve and what she did and how it affected us all. We do not first bring our heart's Question to God and too often, before we can, we are given answers in a very painful way. We are wounded into believing horrid things about ourselves. And so every woman comes into the world set up for a terrible heartbreak.

Let's close our journaling time today with prayer.

> *Dear God, merciful God. I need your help. Please forgive me for the ways that I choose to live that have nothing to do with trusting you. Please come for me. Reveal to me the ways that I live that are not pleasing to you and grant me the grace of a deep and true repentance. Please speak to my deep heart where I need to hear from you. How do you see me? Am I lovely to you? I give you permission to have your way with me. Reveal to me more of who you are God and who I am to you. Thank you. In Jesus' name. Amen.*

CHAPTER FOUR

Wounded

These words are razors to my wounded heart.
—William Shakespeare

Ah, Women, that you should be moving
here, among us, grief-filled,
no more protected than we.
—Rainer Maria Rilke

We opened this chapter in the companion book by telling the story of little Carrie's marvelous sixth birthday and how she was surrounded by parents who loved her deeply, intentionally, and well. She was a little girl who felt wanted and delighted in, cherished by both her mother and her father. Although the story is based on real people with real lives, to many of us, it sounds like a fairy tale.

How did you feel reading about Carrie's birthday morning? Cynical? Longing?

Before we move into this chapter, let's ask Jesus to come.

Dear Jesus, I love you. I need you. I come before you now, once again, as yours, asking for your help, your grace. My life is yours. My heart is yours. Would you please come and shine your light into the depths of my heart that I might understand myself better and come to know your healing and your presence more deeply. Help me to remember what I need to remember. Help me to see, to understand, to repent, to forgive, to heal, and to become. Jesus, I give you access to all of my heart. I invite you into every part. Come, Holy Spirit, have your way . . . that I might love you, God, more deeply and truly with all of my heart, soul, mind, and strength. In Jesus' name I pray. Amen.

Windows to Your Heart

I love the story *A Little Princess* (I talked about it in the book). Did you read it as a girl? You might enjoy it or the recent movie version again. In a way, her story is a reflection of all of our stories.

Now, look back over the chapter, skimming the pages. Did you highlight anything? What strikes you? What did it evoke in your heart?

Mothers, Fathers, and Their Daughters

For many centuries women lived in close fellowships with other women—gathering at the well, down by the river, preparing meals—many occasions for femininity to just sort of naturally pass from older women to younger women. Our intuition, our keen eye for relationship, our ability to grasp matters of the heart made any sort of formal "passage" into femininity unnecessary. . . . The way you see yourself now, as a grown woman, was shaped early in your life, in the years when you were a little girl. We learned what it meant to be feminine—and if we were feminine—while we were very young. Women learn from their mothers what it means to be a woman, and from their fathers the value that a woman has—the value they have as a woman. If a woman is comfortable with her own femininity, her beauty, her strength, then the chances are good that her daughter will be, too.

Was your mother comfortable with her femininity? How would you describe her, as a woman?

Try to put some words to what you learned about femininity from watching your mother.

What did your father value about women? What did you learn from him about femininity? How did (does) he treat your mom?

Mother Wounds

Fallen women tend to sin in one of two ways. Either they become controlling, dominating women or they become mousy, desolate women. Which way would you say your mother tended to sway? What was that like for you?

Our mothers play a huge role in our lives. We will look more at that in a later chapter, but for now, it would be good to journal a little bit about your childhood. What was your childhood like?

Lifting the Veil

To share the story of your life with a trusted friend or two is a powerful experience. We cannot really know others, and they cannot really know us well without understanding the story of our lives. We live and act and hide and even sin in ways that are a result of the story of our lives. In order to find the healing and the life that God so wants for us, we need to understand our own story. In order for others to fully enter into our lives and journey with us and us with them, we need to know each others' stories as well.

Pray. Ask God to bring women into your life that you can trust and journey with. If you already have them, pray about making the time to share your stories with each other.

To share your story, you will need about three hours of uninterrupted time in a safe, comfortable, quiet place. Per person. You will want Kleenex available. Pray together first. Ask God to help you remember what would be good to share and to give you the courage to speak. It is never neatly or perfectly done. But it is very good to begin.

Father Wounds

In the previous chapter we talked a bit about the questions that are birthed in little girls' hearts with their first breath. Little girls, all little girls, want to know if they are delighted in, lovely, wanted. And their question is primarily answered by their father, or if he is absent, by his absence or by other key men in her life.

> We wanted to know, "Daddy, am I lovely? Am I captivating?" From them, we learn that we are delighted in, that we are special—or that we are not. How a father relates to his daughter has an enormous effect on her soul, for good or for evil.

Did your father delight in you? (And I mean in honorable, appropriate ways.) If he did (oh how I hope he did), what about you did he delight in? How did you know it?

Did you know to the core of your being that you were loved, special, worth protecting, and wanted? I pray so. But I know that for many of you, the childhood you were meant to have, the childhood you wanted to have, is a far cry from the childhood you did have. How did your father answer your Question, "*Am I captivating*?"

Is there a defining wound you remember receiving from your father or your mother? What happened?

If, like me, your father *didn't* delight in you as a little girl, try to put some words to what you would have wanted him to say or do.

As we said earlier, fallen men tend to sin in one of two ways. Either they become driven, violent men—their strength gone bad—or they become passive, silent men (like Adam)—their strength gone away.

Which way would you say your father tended to sway? What was that like for you? Any specific memories?

The Messages of Our Wounds—and How They Shaped Us

The wounds that we received as young girls did not come alone. They brought messages with them, messages that struck at the core of our hearts, right in the place of our Question. *Our wounds strike at the core of our femininity.* The damage done to our feminine hearts through the wounds we received is made much worse by the horrible things we believe about ourselves as a result. As children, we didn't have the faculties to process and sort through what was happening to us. Our parents were godlike. We believed them to be right. If we were overwhelmed or belittled or hurt or abused, we believed that somehow it was because of us—the problem was with us.

What do you believe about yourself *as a woman*?

Many of us women feel that, as women, somehow we are not enough. We can't put words to it, but down deep we fear there is something terribly wrong with us. If we had been the princess, then our prince would have come. If we had been the daughter of a king, he would have fought for us. We can't help but believe that if we had been different, if we had been better, then we would have been loved as we so longed to be. It must be us.

Do you feel that way? Believe that there is something at your very core that is wrong with you?

You see, the wounds we received did not come alone. They came with messages that were delivered with such pain we believed the messages were true. My parents did not want me. I was a bother. Simply too much. I believed it. I believed that I was too much, too much trouble and a deep disappointment. And so I made a vow. Somewhere in my young heart I decided that since I was too much, I would do everything I could to not cause pain. I hid. The vows we make as children are very understandable—and very, very damaging. They shut our hearts down. They are essentially a deep-seated agreement with the messages of our wounds. They act as an agreement with the verdict on us. "Fine. If that's how it is, then that's how it is. I'll live my life in the following way . . . "

Does this make sense to you? How did the wounds you received as a little girl shape the way you see yourself as a woman now?

Lifting the Veil

We are speaking of wounds we received when we were young, or at least while we were still a youth in our parents' home. But the assault against our heart continues into adulthood. If you are more aware of wounds that came as a young woman, then journal about those. How have those shaped your view of yourself as a woman?

Can you begin to see the "vows" that you made on how you would live? (Again, ask for God's help here. These things run so deeply inside of us they are difficult to see.) What vows did you make?

Shame

The result of the wounds we received was to make us believe that some part of us, maybe every part of us, is marred. Shame enters in and makes its crippling home deep within our hearts. Shame is what makes us look away, so we avoid eye contact with strangers and friends. Shame is that feeling that haunts us, the sense that if someone really knew us, they would shake their heads in disgust as they ran away. Shame makes us feel, no, believe, that we do not measure up—not to the world's standards, the church's standards, or our own.

Shame causes us to hide. "I was afraid because I was naked; so I hid" (Gen. 3:10 NKJV).

Do you ever feel this? In what ways are you aware of that you are hiding these days?

An Unholy Alliance

The only thing more tragic than the things that have happened to us is what we have done with them.

Words were said; painful words. Things were done; awful things. And they shaped us. Something inside of us shifted. We embraced the messages of our wounds. We accepted a twisted view of ourselves. And from that we chose a way of relating to our world. We made a vow never to be in that place again. We adopted strategies to protect ourselves from being hurt again.

The problem is that our plan has nothing to do with God.

The wounds we received and the messages they brought formed a sort of unholy alliance with our fallen nature as women. From Eve we received a deep mistrust in the heart of God towards us. Clearly, he's holding out on us. We'll just have to arrange for the life we want. We will control our world. But there is also an ache deep within, an ache for intimacy and for life. We'll have to find a way to fill it. A way that does not require us to trust anyone, especially God. A way that will not require vulnerability.

In some ways, this is every little girl's story, here in this world east of Eden.

Are you aware of a mistrust of God deep in your heart?

Are you aware of ways that you are trying to control your world?

Are there times when you feel an ache and a longing for more intimacy and more life? (That's good, by the way.)

God has much more freedom to move within us when we are honest with him and with ourselves. We'll close this chapter with prayer but before we do, let's recognize together that we don't stop getting wounded once we grow up. In fact, some of our deepest wounds come later in life.

The wounds you have received have landed in your heart in a very similar place. They have a *theme* to them. They came with a purpose, an intention to cripple your glory. In the next chapter we will begin to expose the enemy of your soul who was behind many of your wounds because he knows in part all that you are meant to be and fears you.

Let's pray.

> *Holy and blessed Trinity. You know me. You are familiar with all my ways. Please help me. Revisiting the wounds of my past is so hard. I don't want to feel that pain again. Please come into those places in my heart that remain wounded and hold me there. Heal me there. And in your mercy, please reveal to me the vows I made; the ways I do not trust you. Forgive me and help me to grow in trusting you ever more truly. Please reveal to me more of who you are and who I am to you. In Jesus' name. Amen.*

Recommended reading: So many of us were sexually abused when we were young. If that is part of your story, we highly recommend Dan Allender's *The Wounded Heart* and its accompanying workbook to help you on your road to healing.

CHAPTER FIVE

A Special Hatred

All who hate me whisper about me,
imagining the worst for me.
—PSALM 41:7 NLT

Take away this murdherin' hate, an' give us
Thine own eternal love.
—SEAN O'CASEY

In the companion book we began this chapter by telling the story of the cruel hailstorm that ravaged my once beautiful garden and left behind brokenness, debris, and sorrow. The destruction the storm caused felt like a mini passion play, a picture of the intentional assault against the daughters of Eve.

This chapter asks us to reexamine our thoughts about the often brutal, nearly universal assault on femininity. Where does this come from?

Do not make the mistake of believing that "men are the enemy." Certainly men have had a hand in this and will have a day of reckoning before their Maker. But you will not understand this story—or your story—until you begin to see the actual Forces behind this assault and get a grip on their motives.

Let's begin with prayer.

> *Dear Jesus, I love you. I need you. I come before you now, once again, as yours, asking for your help, your grace. My life is yours. My heart is yours. Would you please come and shine your light into the depths of my heart and into my past that I might understand myself better and come to know your healing and your presence more deeply. Help me to remember what I need to remember. Help me to see, to understand, to repent, to forgive, and to become. Jesus, I give you access to all of my heart. I invite you into every part. Give me all the courage and wisdom and understanding that I need to expose the schemes of the devil. Come, Holy Spirit, have your way . . . that I might love you, God, more deeply, freely, and truly with all of my heart, soul, mind, and strength. In Jesus' name I pray. Amen.*

Windows to Your Heart

In this chapter John pointed out how in nearly every story, the villain goes after the Beauty. It's true of stories from *Cinderella* and *The Little Mermaid* to *Braveheart* and *Titanic*. Think again about the stories that you love. Who is the villain? Does he (or she) at some point attack the Beauty? Why? (It might help to watch one of those again, and this time, put yourself in the role of the Beauty.) Also, if you've never watched *Ever After*, you might really enjoy it in connection with your work here.

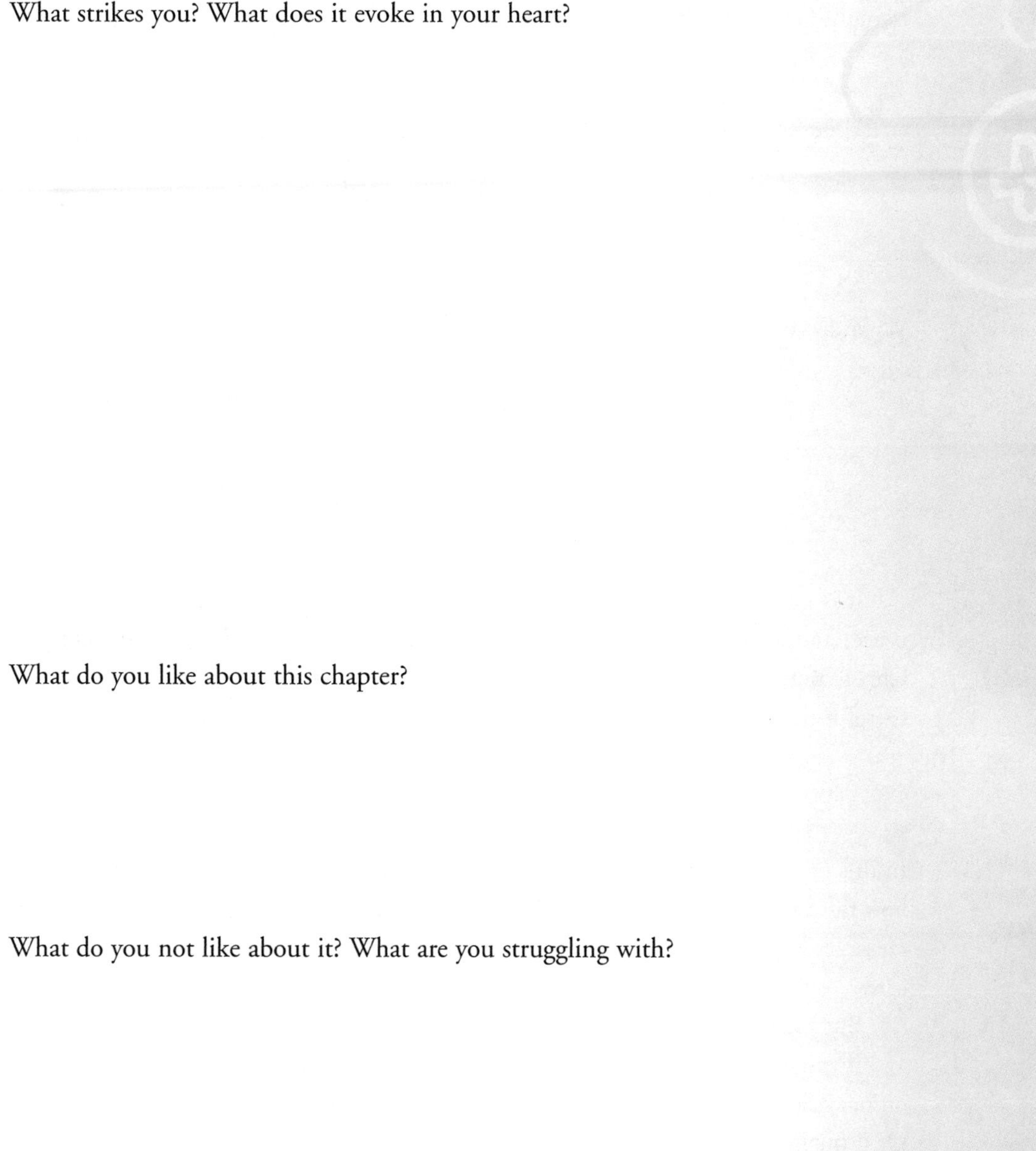

Now, go back over the chapter, skimming the pages. Did you highlight anything? What strikes you? What does it evoke in your heart?

What do you like about this chapter?

What do you not like about it? What are you struggling with?

Is it a new thought to you that all that has come against you in your life has not been from the hand of God? That Satan has played a role in trying to destroy you, your heart?

What do you do with that?

It is good to remember that God has not given us a spirit of fear, but of love, peace, and a sound mind. We do not need to fear the enemy. We have victory in Christ. But, we do need to expose his tactics and learn how to take a stand against them in the truth of God's Word. (More on that in Chapter 11.)

Further Assault

In this part of the book, I shared with you the story of sexual assault against me and how the assault painfully reinforced messages from my childhood wounds. For me the messages were "Hide your heart. You are a disappointment. You are worthless. No one cares. You are alone." And it felt that it was my fault.

But I have come to know that I am not alone in this.

If you will listen carefully to any woman's story, you will hear a theme: The assault on her heart. It might be obvious as in the stories of physical, verbal, or sexual abuse. Or it might be more subtle, the indifference of a world that cares nothing for her but uses her until she is drained. Forty years of being neglected damages a woman's heart, too, dear friends. Either way, the wounds continue to come long after we've "grown up," but they all seem to speak the same message. Our Question is answered again and again throughout our life, the message driven home into our hearts like a stake.

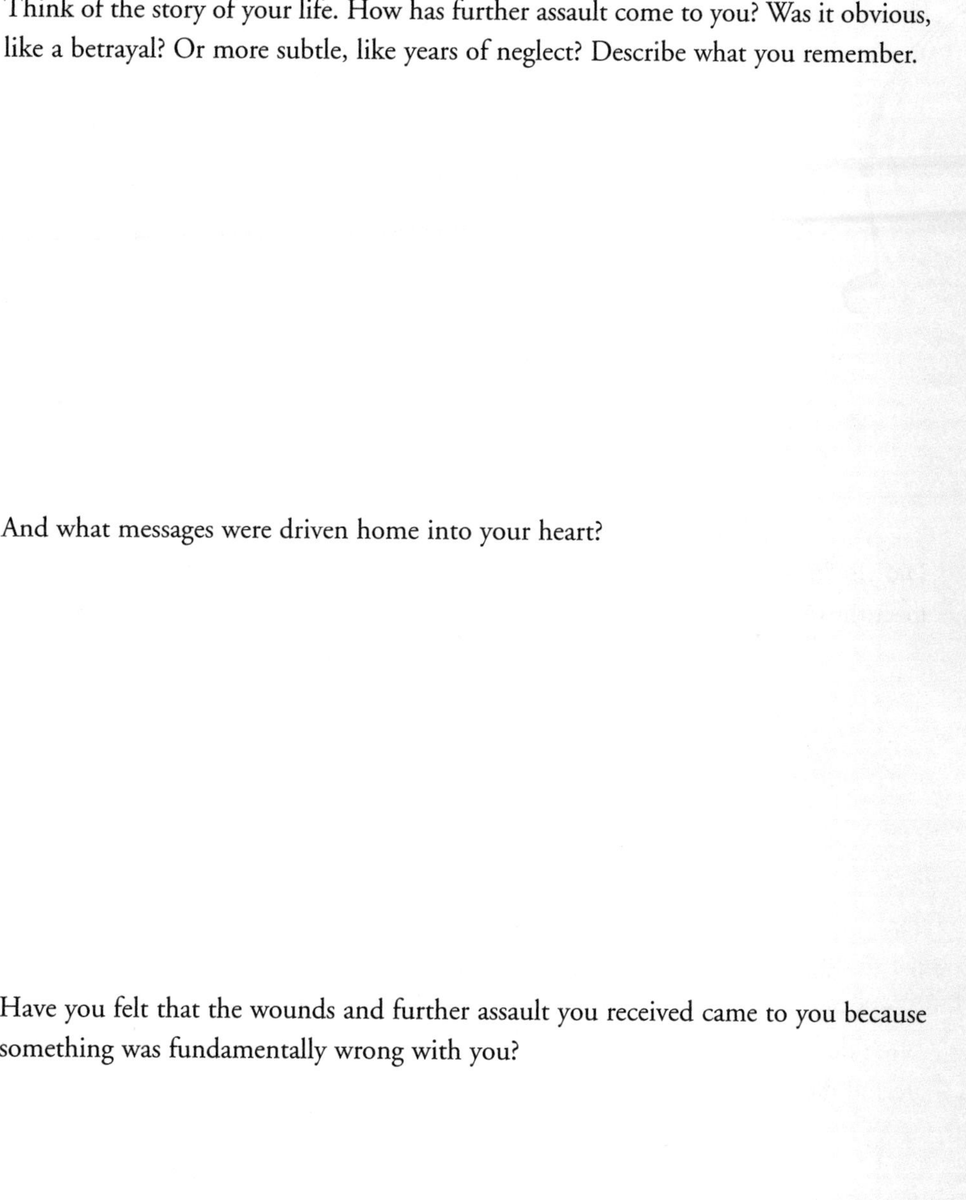

Think of the story of your life. How has further assault come to you? Was it obvious, like a betrayal? Or more subtle, like years of neglect? Describe what you remember.

And what messages were driven home into your heart?

Have you felt that the wounds and further assault you received came to you because something was fundamentally wrong with you?

Have you felt that you are essentially alone? If you do, do you believe it is because you are not the woman you should be?

Did you know that most women feel essentially alone? (I won't say all, but I've yet to meet the one who doesn't.)

What Is Really Going On Here?

The story of the treatment of women down through the ages is not a noble history. It has noble moments in it, to be sure, but taken as a whole, women have endured what seems to be a special hatred ever since we left Eden.

What do you make of the degradation, the abuse, and the open assault that women around the world have endured? Are enduring even now?

Where does this hatred for women you see all over the world come from? Why is it so diabolical?

Well, how *have* you explained all this?

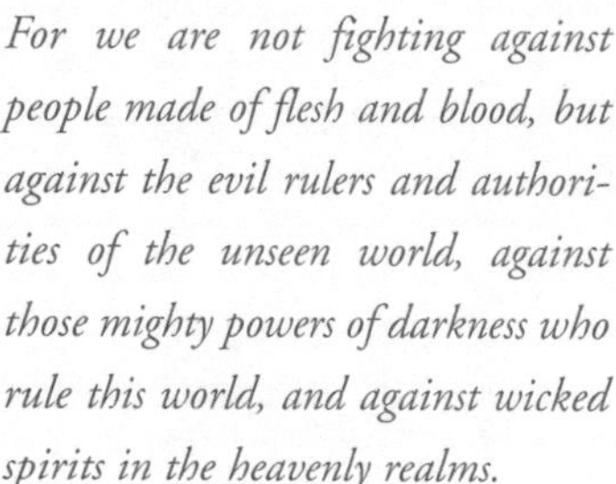

For we are not fighting against people made of flesh and blood, but against the evil rulers and authorities of the unseen world, against those mighty powers of darkness who rule this world, and against wicked spirits in the heavenly realms.

—EPHESIANS 6:12 NLT

A SPECIAL HATRED

The assault on femininity—its long history, its utter viciousness—cannot be understood apart from the spiritual forces of evil we are warned against in the Scriptures. This is not to say that men (and women, for they, too, assault women) have no accountability in their treatment of women. Not at all. It is simply to say that no explanation for the assault upon Eve and her daughters is sufficient unless it opens our eyes to the Prince of Darkness and his special hatred of femininity.

Turn your attention again to the events that took place in the Garden of Eden. Notice—who does the Evil One go after?

Have you ever wondered why Satan seems to make Eve the focus of his assault on humanity?

Satan was first named Lucifer, or Son of the Morning. It infers a glory, a brightness, a radiance unique to him. Look up Ezek. 28:12–15. How does it describe Lucifer?

What happened? (See Ezek. 28:17.)

Satan's heart became proud. He no longer wanted to be Best Supporting Actor; he wanted all the glory for himself.

> Satan fell because of his beauty. Now his heart for revenge is to assault beauty. He destroys it in the natural world wherever he can. Strip mines, oil spills, fires, Chernobyl. He wreaks destruction on the glory of God in the earth like a psychopath committed to destroying great works of art.

What are some other examples of Satan's destruction? When the devil has his way with the world, what are some examples of the results?

But What of Eve?

She is the incarnation of the Beauty of God. More than anything else in all creation, she embodies the glory of God. She allures the world to God. Satan hates it with a jealousy we can only imagine.

And there is more. The Evil One also hates Eve because she gives life. Women give birth, not men. Women nourish life. And they also bring life into the world soulfully, relationally, spiritually—in everything they touch.

Put those two things together—Eve incarnates the Beauty of God, and she gives life to the world. Satan's bitter heart cannot bear it. He assaults her with a special hatred. History removes any doubt about this.

Do you begin to see it?

It is even in the great stories—the villain goes after the Hero's true love, the Beauty. Can you think of some?

Satan's hatred of Eve and her daughters helps to explain an awful lot about your life's story. The message of our wounds nearly always is, "This is because of you. This is what you deserve." It changes things to realize that no, these things happened because you are glorious, because you are a major threat to the kingdom of darkness. Because you uniquely carry the glory of God to the world.

You are hated *because* of your beauty and power.

Do you believe that could be possible?

Do you believe it is possible for your women friends?

If it could be true of them, could it not be true of you as well?

Let your imagination go there a little while. What would it feel like if it were true that you *are* beautiful, that you *are* powerful for the kingdom of God—and that is why you have endured the assault (and neglect) you have?

On a Human Level

In this section, John was honest about his hesitancy to enter more fully into the world of women that writing *Captivating* with me would require. (As part of his further induction, I invited him to watch several "women" films with me. He gamely did and then needed me to explain them to him. "What was *that* about?")

He also wrote about a deeper feeling that he sensed around women: A sense that was more like an allergic reaction to Back Off. Withdraw. Pull back. Pull away.

Have you ever felt the men in your life get close only to withdraw, pull back? What happened? Who did you blame it on?

Have you felt from men that you are too hard, too much trouble, too complicated, as a woman?

If you are married or in a close relationship with a man, are you aware of an unspoken settlement, something like your man saying, "I'm not coming any closer. This is as far as I'm willing to go. But, I won't leave, and that ought to make you happy." Is there a sort of détente, a cordial agreement to live only so close?

Some of this is simply selfishness, weakness on the part of men. But there is something more. There is something diabolical at work here. Often when men do "back off" from their women, it is because they feel a strong pull to do so. A strong impression to end the conversation; to not press in any further, that it would be better for everyone if they withdrew.

Want to risk asking the man in your life if he has felt that? Do you already know the answer? If you do ask him, then ask if he withdrew because he thought it was what you wanted him to do.

Back off, or *Leave her alone,* or *You don't really want to go there—she'll be too much for you* is something Satan has set against every woman from the day of her birth. It's the emotional and spiritual equivalent of leaving a little girl by the side of the road to die. And to every woman he has whispered, You are alone, or When they see who you really are, you will be alone, or No one will ever truly come for you.

Take a moment. Quiet your heart and ask yourself, "Is this a message I have believed, feared, lived with?"

Not only do most women fear they will eventually be abandoned by the men in their lives—they fear it from other women as well. That they will be abandoned by their friends and left alone. It's time to reveal this pervasive threat as the tool of the Enemy that it is.

Remember the scene in *The Two Towers*, second film in the *Lord of the Rings* trilogy, where Wormtongue haunts Eowyn with threats that she is alone? She is victorious over his lies when she refuses to believe them.

Wormtongue: "O, but you are alone. Who knows what you have spoken to the darkness in bitter watches of the night when all your life seems to shrink, the walls of your bower closing in about you. A hushed, tremulsome, wild thing."(He takes her face in his hand.) "So fair . . . and so cold. Like a morning with pale spring, still clinging to winter's chill."

Eowyn replies as we must. "Your words are poison."

How long have you been living with a fear of abandonment? How much of your efforts to "be a good woman" or to make yourself beautiful are fueled by that fear?

There Is Hope

I (John) am not letting men off the hook. God knows we have a lot more repenting to do. I am saying that you won't begin to understand the long and sustained assault on femininity, on women, until you see it as part of something much larger: The most wicked force the world has ever known. The Enemy bears a special hatred for Eve. If you believe he has any role in the history of this world, you cannot help but see it.

Are you beginning to see it?

The Evil One had a hand in all that has happened to you. If he didn't arrange for the assault directly—and certainly human sin has a large enough role to play—then he made sure he drove the message of the wounds home into your heart. He is the one who has dogged your heels with shame and self-doubt and accusation. He is the one who offers the false comforters to you in order to deepen your bondage. He is the one who has done these things in order to prevent your restoration. For that is what he fears. He fears who you are, what you are—what you might become. He fears your beauty and your life-giving heart.

What if it were true? How does that make you feel?

Now, listen to the voice of your King.

Read Isaiah 62:1–5. If you can, read it in more than one translation.

Who is Jerusalem?

What are you no longer called?

What are you called?

Read Jeremiah 30:16–17.

How will God treat your enemies?

How will he treat you?

You really won't understand your life as a woman until you understand this:

You are passionately loved by the God of the universe.
You are passionately hated by his Enemy.

Are you beginning to believe it?

And so, dear heart, it is time for your restoration. For there is One greater than your Enemy. One who has sought you out from the beginning of time. He has come to heal your broken heart and restore your feminine soul. Let us turn now to Him.

Dear Jesus, I am beginning to see the assault on my life and on my heart, as coming from the enemy. He has been fierce against me. I have been wounded and wounded deeply. And I am trying to believe, beginning to believe, that it was not all my fault. Not what I deserved. Oh, God, please come to my battered heart and heal me. Come to the places in my heart where I have believed the enemy's lies to me for so long and speak the truth to me, there. In those places. I need you. I need your protection. I need your mercy. I need your covering, your kindness, and your touch. Make me quick to recognize the ploys of the enemy and teach me to stand against them. Please come for me, Jesus. And heal me. In your name, I pray. Amen.

CHAPTER SIX

Healing the Wound

I didn't know just what was wrong with me,
Till your love helped me name it.
—ARETHA FRANKLIN

Down those old ancient streets,
Down those old ancient roads,
Baby there together we must go
Till we get the healing done.
—VAN MORRISON

We began the book's companion chapter with a retelling of the story of our son Blaine's rescue of a wounded, confused, beautiful hummingbird. We were so concerned for this little flying jewel's welfare. As you read the story, were you concerned as well?

Jesus said, don't you think God cares just a little bit more for you than for the birds of the air? "Are you not much more valuable than they?" (Matt. 6:26 NKJV). Indeed, you are. You, dear heart, are the crown of creation, his glorious image bearer. And he will do everything it takes to rescue you, and set your heart free.

Let us ask him to come and to help us now.

Dear Jesus, I love you. I need you. I come before you now, once again, as yours, asking for your help, your grace, your courage. My life is yours. My heart is yours. Would you please come and tenderly hold my heart as together, with you, I go through this chapter? I long to know your healing and your presence more deeply. Help me be kind to my heart. Help me remember what I need to remember. Help me to see, to understand, to grieve, to forgive, and to be healed. Jesus, I give you access to all of my heart. I invite you into every part. Come, Holy Spirit, have your way . . . that I might love you, God, more deeply and truly with all of my heart, soul, mind, and strength. In Jesus' name I pray. Amen.

Windows to Your Heart

In Tolkien's third book *The Return of the King*, Aragorn, the Christ figure, is moved to tend the wounded in the Houses of Healing.

Then Gandalf said: "Let us not stay at the door, for the time is urgent. Let us enter! For it is only in the coming of Aragorn that any hope remains for the sick that lie in the House. Thus spake Ioreth, the wise-woman of Gondor: The hands of the king are the hands of a healer, and so shall the rightful king be known."

Yes. There is healing in the hands of our King.

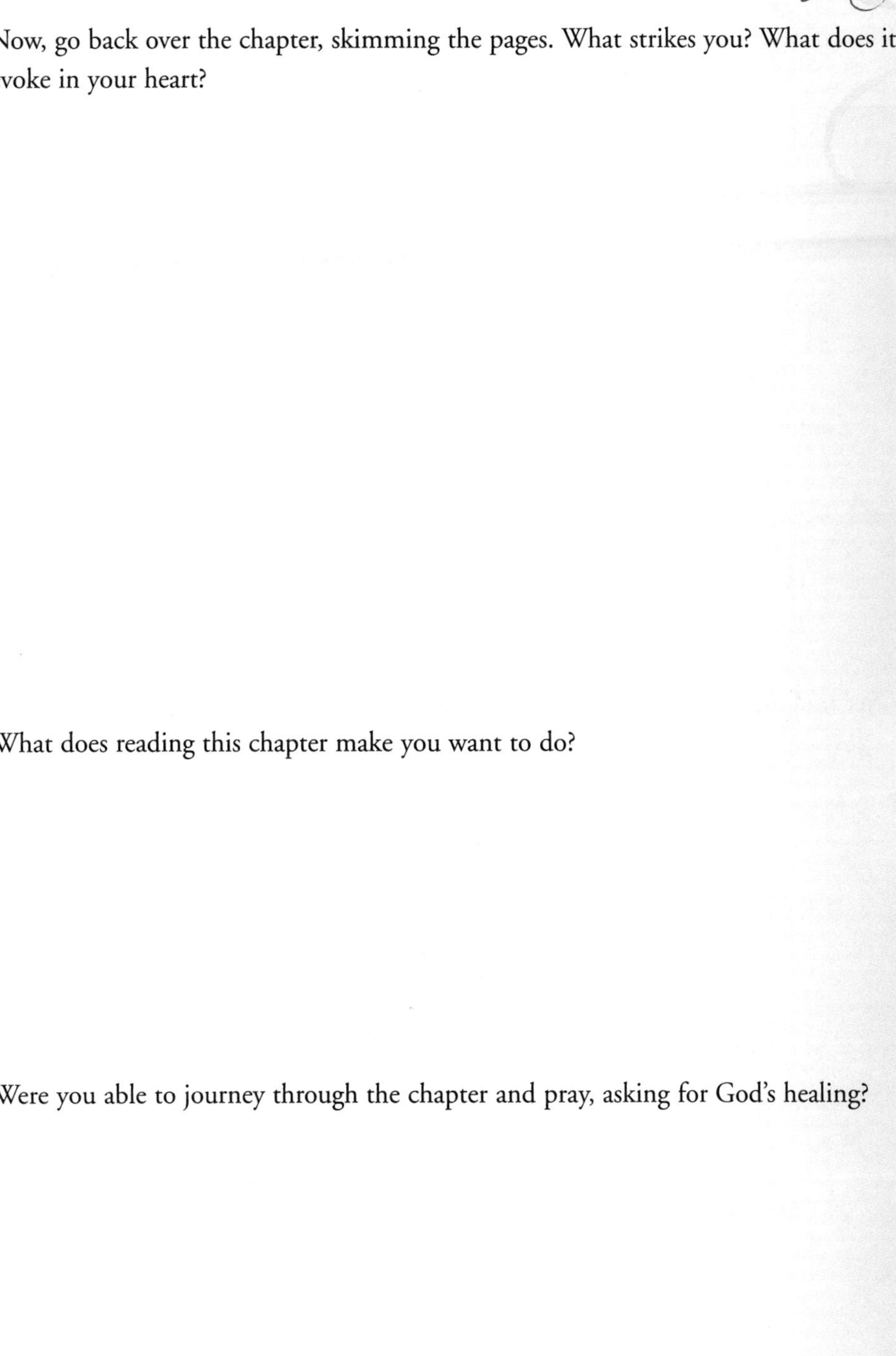

Now, go back over the chapter, skimming the pages. What strikes you? What does it evoke in your heart?

What does reading this chapter make you want to do?

Were you able to journey through the chapter and pray, asking for God's healing?

What in your heart do you really want him to heal, touch, and restore?

Ask him again.

> *Jesus, come to me and heal my heart. Come to the shattered places within me. Come for the little girl that was wounded. Come and hold me in your arms and heal me. Do for me what you promised to do—heal my broken heart and set me free.*

After reading this chapter on Healing, what are you struggling with?

What, if anything, presented in this chapter are you having a hard time believing?

Lifting the Veil

We all need Jesus to come for us. And we never stop needing him to come, to touch, to heal, and to restore our hearts. The journey of becoming ever more healed, ever more his, is such an important one, we think it would be good to take the time your heart needs and walk through this chapter slowly, carefully, with God tenderly holding your heart.

What we lay out here is a sort of step-by-step process for healing, one that we've found helpful in our own lives. It is not a formula. God may bring other things up as you pray through this. Go with the guidance of the Holy Spirit. And rest assured that he wants to heal, and will come and heal. Sometimes in a moment. Sometimes over the course of months and years.

The Offer

What have you been taught is the primary reason that Jesus came to earth?

Jesus proclaims his mission when he takes the scroll of Isaiah and begins his public ministry. What passage did he choose to explain himself? (Isaiah 61)

Listen to this passage from Isaiah (it might help to read it very slowly, carefully, aloud to yourself):

The Spirit of the Sovereign Lord is on me,
because the Lord has anointed me
to preach good news to the poor.
He has sent me to bind up the brokenhearted,
to proclaim freedom for the captives
and release from darkness for the prisoners,
to proclaim the year of the Lord's favor
and the day of vengeance of our God,
to comfort all who mourn,
and provide for those who grieve in Zion—
to bestow on them a crown of beauty
instead of ashes,
the oil of gladness
instead of mourning,
and a garment of praise
instead of a spirit of despair.

—Isaiah 61:1–3 NKJV

This Scripture must be important to him. It must be central. What does it mean? It's supposed to be really good news; that's clear. It has something to do with healing hearts, setting someone free. Let me try and state it in words more familiar to us. (It's helpful to read this aloud as well.)

God has sent me on a mission.
I have some great news for you.
God has sent me to restore and release something.
And that something is you.
I am here to give you back your heart and set you free.
I am furious at the Enemy who did this to you, and I will fight against him.
Let me comfort you.
For, dear one, I will bestow beauty upon you
where you have known only devastation.

Joy, in the places of your deep sorrow.
And I will robe your heart in thankful praise
in exchange for your resignation and despair.

Now that is an offer worth considering. In your own words, what is the offer?

What if it were true? What if Jesus could and would do this for your broken heart, your wounded feminine soul?

Read it again and ask him,

Jesus, would you do this for me?

He can, and he will. If you'll let him. The Son of God has come to ransom you, and to heal your broken, wounded, bleeding heart and to set you free from bondage. He came for the brokenhearted captives. That's me. That's you. He came to restore the glorious creation that you are. And then to set you free—to be yourself.

Here is the core reason we wrote this book: To let you know that the healing of your feminine heart is available and to help you find that healing. To help you find the restoration which we long for and which is central to Jesus' mission. Let him take you by the hand now and walk with you through your restoration and release.

Hemmed In

Why did God curse Eve with loneliness and heartache, an emptiness that nothing would be able to fill? Wasn't her life going to be hard enough out there in the world, banished from the Garden that was her true home, her only home, never able to return? It seems unkind. Cruel, even.

He did it to *save* her. For as we all know personally, something in Eve's heart shifted at the Fall. Something sent its roots down deep into her soul—and ours—that mistrust of God's heart, that resolution to find life on our own terms. So God has to thwart her. In love, he has to block her attempts until, wounded and aching;, she turns to him and him alone for her rescue.

> *Therefore I will block her path with thornbushes;*
> *I will wall her in so she cannot find her way.*
> *She will chase after her lovers but not catch them;*
> *she will look for them but not find them.*
>
> —Hosea 2:6–7 NKJV

Jesus has to thwart us, too—thwart our self-redemptive plans, our controlling and our hiding, and thwart the ways we are seeking to fill the ache within us. Otherwise, we would never fully turn to him for our rescue. Oh, we might turn to him for our "salvation," for a ticket to heaven when we die. We might turn to him even in the form of Christian service, regular church attendance, a moral life. But *inside*, our heart would remain broken and captive and far from the One who can help us.

And so you will see the gentle, firm hand of God in a woman's life hemming her in. He'll make what once was a great job miserable, if it were in her career that she found shelter. He'll bring hardship into her marriage, even to the breaking point, if it were in marriage she sought her salvation. Wherever it is, woman has sought life apart from him, he disrupts her plans, her "way of life" which is not life at all.

Okay—what *hasn't* been going well in your life for sometime? Has it occurred to you that God might be "blocking your path with thornbushes" (Hos. 2:6)? How is he thwarting you?

Lifting the Veil

Now, listen carefully: Not every distress in our life is brought by our God. We don't believe even most of them are. We have an enemy. If Jesus warns us that Satan comes to steal, kill, and destroy (John 10:10), then he does. Don't assume the obstacles are always from God.

Ask God to show you where he has been thwarting you, blocking your path. Wherever it is we have sought life apart from him, he will disrupt our plans. Life apart from God will not work. He is thwarting you because he loves you.

Reread Susan's story. Do you see how her plan to save herself stemmed from how she was wounded? How has the way you have been wounded shaped the way you have chosen to live, to protect yourself from being wounded again?

Turning from the Ways You've Sought to Save Yourself

Lifting the Veil

Frederick Buechner says, "To do for yourself the best that you have it in you to do—to grit your teeth and clench your fists in order to survive the world at its harshest and worst—is, by that very act, to be unable to let something be done for you and in you that is more wonderful still. The trouble with steeling yourself against the harshness of reality is that the same steel that secures your life against being destroyed secures your life also against being opened up and transformed. . . ." *(The Sacred Journey).*

Change a few of the details and you have my story—and yours. We construct a life of safety ("I will not be vulnerable there") and find some place to get a taste of being enjoyed, or at least, of being "needed." Our journey towards healing begins when we repent of those ways, lay them down, let them go. They've been a royal disaster anyway. God comes to us and asks, "Will you let me come for you?" Not only does he thwart, but at the same time he calls to us as he did to our friend Susan, "Set it down. Set it down. Turn from your ways to me. I want to come for you."

Therefore I am now going to allure her;
I will lead her into the desert
and speak tenderly to her.
—Hosea 2:14 NKJV

To enter the journey towards the healing of your feminine heart, all it requires is a "Yes. Okay." A simple turning in the heart. Like the Prodigal we wake one day to see that the life we've constructed is no life at all. We let desire speak to us again; we let our hearts have a voice, and what the voice usually says is, this isn't working. My life is a disaster. Jesus—I'm sorry. Forgive me. Please come for me.

Are you ready and willing to say this to Jesus? Perhaps in a deeper way than ever before? If you are, then go ahead and say it. Be specific—what do you need to lay down? Repent of? Let go?

> *Jesus, I'm sorry. Forgive me. Please come for me. I renounce the ways I've tried to save myself. They have failed. Only you can save me. Please come for me. I give this all to you.*

Invite Him In

There is a famous passage of Scripture that many people have heard in the context of an invitation to know Christ as Savior. "Behold, I stand at the door and knock. If anyone hears My voice and opens the door, I will come in . . . " (Rev. 3:20 NKJV). The principle of this "knocking and waiting for permission to come in" remains true well into our Christian life.

It might come as a surprise that Christ asks our permission to come in and heal, but he is kind, and the door is shut from the inside, and healing never comes against our will. In order to experience his healing we must also give him permission to come in to the places we have so long shut to anyone. Will you let me heal you? He knocks through our loneliness. He knocks through our sorrows. He knocks through events that feel too close to what happened to us when we were young—a betrayal, a rejection, a word is spoken, a relationship is lost. He knocks through many things, waiting for us to give him permission to enter in.

What is God "knocking" through these days? Think of the way your life is not working out—or the lives of women you look at and long for. How is God stirring your heart?

Give him permission to enter. Give him access to your broken heart. Ask him to come to these places.

> *Yes, Jesus, yes. I do invite you in. Come to my heart in these shattered places. (You know what they are—ask him there. Is it the abuse? The loss of your father? The jealousy of your mother? Ask him in). Come to me, my Savior. I open this door of my heart. I give you permission to heal my wounds. Come to me here. Come for me here.*

Sit quietly a while. Rest. Wait. Journal your thoughts, feelings, desires.

Renounce the Agreements You've Made

Your wounds brought messages with them. Lots of messages. Somehow they all usually land in the same place. They had a similar theme. Because they were delivered with such pain, they *felt* true.

What theme would you say was delivered to your heart via the wounds you have received? What "messages" have dogged you all these years? What did you come to believe about yourself? Sometimes we need God's help to uncover what we really believe. Ask Jesus, *Lord, show me what I've believed about myself all these years. What is my image of myself? What lies have I held onto?* Write them down.

The beliefs we hold about ourselves based on the wounds we received become a deep seated agreement with the message of our wounds. From that, we make vows, decisions on how we will then live. Those childhood vows are very dangerous things. We must renounce them. *Before we are entirely convinced that they aren't true, we must reject the message of our wounds.* It's a way of unlocking the door to Jesus. Agreements lock the door from the inside. Renouncing the agreements unlocks the door to him.

Jump in. If you feel ready or not, let Jesus in.

> *Jesus, forgive me for embracing these lies. This is not what you have said of me. You said I am your daughter, your beloved, your cherished one. I renounce the agreements I made with (name the specific messages you've been living with. "I'm stupid." " I'm ugly." You know what they are). I renounce the agreements I've been making with these messages all these years. Bring the truth here, Oh Spirit of Truth. I reject these lies.*

We Find Our Tears

Part of the reason women are so tired is because we are spending so much energy trying to "keep it together." So much energy devoted to suppressing the pain and keeping a good appearance.

We want to give you permission to fall apart. To be a mess.

Does that thought frighten you? Why?

We need to let our tears come. Give yourself permission to feel, to sorrow. Make the time. Get alone, get to your car or your bedroom or the shower and let the tears come. Let the tears come. It is the only kind thing to do for your woundedness. Allow yourself to feel again. And feel you will—many things. Let it all out.

Lifting the Veil

When I (Stasi) really began to feel my sorrow, I was afraid the pain would overwhelm me. I was afraid that if I let myself begin to cry, I would never be able to stop. I felt embarrassed to cry in front of others. I felt ashamed of my tears and somehow deserving of grief. But once we begin the journey of healing, God is tender and cunning to lance our wounds. He wants us to feel. He wants to draw near as we grieve. For me, I needed privacy in order to let my tears come. The only place I could find that in that time of my life was in the shower, water running full blast. And there, I invited God into my sorrow and risked feeling my pain, letting my tears run freely.

Forgive

Okay—now for a hard step (as if the others have been easy). A real step of courage and will. We must forgive those who hurt us.

Again.

Until you forgive, you remain their prisoner. Paul warns us that unforgiveness and bitterness can wreck our lives and the lives of others (Eph. 4:31; Heb. 12:15). We have to let it all go.

Who do you still hold in your heart in anger, resentment, unforgiveness? Be honest.

Now—listen carefully. Forgiveness is a choice. It is not a feeling—don't try and feel forgiving. It is an act of the will. "Don't wait to forgive until you feel like forgiving," wrote Neil Anderson. "You will never get there. Feelings take time to heal after the choice to forgive is made . . ." We have to allow God to bring the hurt up from our pasts, for "if your forgiveness doesn't visit the emotional core of your life, it will be incomplete," said Anderson. We acknowledge that it hurt, that it mattered, and we choose to extend forgiveness to our fathers, our mothers, those who hurt us. This is not saying, "It didn't really matter"; it is not saying, "I probably deserved part of it anyway." Forgiveness says, "It was wrong. Very wrong. It mattered, hurt me deeply. And I release you. I give you to God."

It might help to remember that those who hurt you were also deeply wounded themselves. Can you see that in them, in their life story?

Pray now. Let them go. Release them to God. Who are they? What are you forgiving them for?

> *Jesus, thank you for forgiving me. For the price you paid to forgive me. I choose now to forgive those who have hurt me. I forgive (name them) for (name what they did). I release them to you God. You are the just judge. You will deal with them. I cannot be their judge. I let them go, and I choose to forgive.*

Ask Jesus to Heal You

We turn from our self-redemptive strategies. We open the door of our hurting heart to Jesus. We renounce the agreements we made with the messages of our wounds, renounce any vows we made. We forgive those who harmed us. And then, with an open heart, we simply ask Jesus to heal us.

Healing is available. This is the offer of our Savior—to heal our broken hearts. To come to the young places within us and find us there, take us in his arms, bring us home. The time has come to let Jesus heal you. Pray.

> *Jesus, come to me and heal my heart. Come to the shattered places within me. Come for the little girl that was wounded. Come and hold me in your arms and heal me. Do for me what you promised to do—heal my broken heart and set me free.*

Sit quietly. Perhaps journal a little bit. And rest assured that Jesus has heard your cry, has come for you, and will continue to come. Listen for his voice. What is he saying to you?

Ask Him to Destroy Your Enemies

In the beautiful passage from Isaiah 61, God promises "freedom for the captives and release from darkness for the prisoners" (v. 1 NKJV). He goes on to proclaim "vengeance" against our enemies (v. 2 NKJV). Our wounds, our vows, and the agreements we've made with the messages all give ground to the Enemy in our lives. Paul warns about this in Ephesians 4 when he says—writing to Christians—"and do not give the devil a foothold" (Eph 4:27 NKJV). There are things you've struggled with all your life—self-doubt, anger, depression, shame, addiction, fear. You probably thought that those were just your fault, too.

But they are not. They came from the Enemy who wanted to take your heart captive, make you a prisoner of darkness. To be sure, we complied. We allowed those strongholds to form when we mishandled our wounds and made those vows. But Jesus has forgiven us for all of that, and now he wants to set us free.

What enemies of your soul would you like Jesus to destroy? Self contempt? An addiction? A spirit of overwhelmed?

Read Psalm 21:8–13. Ask him to destroy your enemies, the ones you recognize and the one yet to be revealed.

Jesus, come and rescue me. Set me free from [you know what you need freedom from—name it]. Release me from darkness. Bring your vengeance on my enemies. I reject them. I reject the agreements I have made with them. I renounce any permission I have given them in my life. I banish them. And I ask you, Jesus, to take them to judgment. Set my heart free. May your Spirit come and take the place they have held in my life.

Let Him Father You

Then he went with Sara into her little sitting room and they bade each other good-bye. Sara sat on his knee and held the lapels of his coat in her small hands, and looked long and hard at his face.

"Are you learning me by heart, little Sara?" he said, stroking her hair.

"No," she answered. "I know you by heart. You are inside my heart." And they put their arms round each other and kissed as if they would never let each other go.

—Frances Hodgson Burnett, *A Little Princess*

There is a part of our hearts that was made for Daddy; made for his strong and tender love. That part is still there, and longing. Open it to Jesus, and to your Father God. Ask him to come and love you there. Meet you there. We've all tried so hard to find the fulfillment of this love in other people, and it never, ever works. Let us give this treasure back to the One who can love us best.

Father, I need your love. Come to the core of my heart. Come and bring your love for me. Help me to know you for who you really are—not as I see my earthly father. Reveal yourself to me. Reveal your love for me. Tell me what I mean to you. Come, and father me here, in the lost and lonely and wounded places of my heart.

Ask Him to Answer Your Question

In the story of *A Little Princess,* Sara has a deep rooted confidence that she is loved. She is special. She is, in fact, a true princess, regardless of her circumstances or appearance. She says to herself, "Whatever comes, cannot alter one thing. If I am a princess in rags and tatters, I can be a princess inside. It would be easy to be a princess if I were dressed in a cloth of gold, but it is a great deal more of a triumph to be one all the time when no one knows it." How did she come to such a confidence?

How do we come to such a confidence? We take our heart's deepest Question to God. You still have a Question, dear one. We all do. We all still need to know, Do you see me? Am I captivating? Do I have a beauty all my own?

Let's just start with a thought. What if the message delivered with your wounds simply isn't true about you? Let that sink in. Ponder that. It wasn't true. What does it free you to do? Weep? Rejoice? Let go? Come out? Take your heart back?

Now, take your questions to Jesus. Ask him to show you your beauty.

Dear Jesus, I am almost afraid to ask, but I so need the answer. I need the questions of my deepest heart answered. And answered truthfully. Answered by you. Lord, how do you see me? As a woman. Am I captivating to you? Am I lovely? Would you please show me my beauty? Show me what you think of me. I want to hear from you. Open the eyes of my heart that I may recognize and receive your answers as you bring them to me. I need to know God. I will wait and listen. For I love you, and my heart is yours. All this I pray, in the name of Jesus. Amen.

Lifting the Veil

Healing is a journey. God comes, and he heals deep wounds in our hearts. Then, several months later, he reveals another wound, or wounds. So we go through this process again. We invite Jesus in. We renounce our childhood vows. We forgive. We ask him to heal. John and I have been walking this path for years, and we can promise you—God really does come and restore the hearts of his beloved.

For Further Reading: To help you in your journey towards deeper healing, may we also recommend John's book, *Waking the Dead*—especially chapters six through ten.

CHAPTER SEVEN

Romanced

I have loved you with an everlasting love.
—God (Jeremiah 31:3 NKJV)

Romance is the deepest thing in life.
It is deeper even than reality.
—G.K. Chesterton

What do you think the G.K. Chesterton quote means?

I am sighing as I begin this part of the journal. The truth that what God—the Ageless Romancer—wants most from us is our heart's love; that he is captivated by *us* is almost too marvelous for words. He sees something in us that we don't yet see. It is hard to grasp that we are extravagantly loved by the God of the Universe. But it is *true.* And that is just the best news, the most glorious reality.

Having our hearts begin to grasp the depth of Jesus' personal, intimate, intentional love for us, changes us. In all the best ways.

We need his help here. We need revelation from him about his love of us.

Dear Jesus, I love you. I need you. I come before you now as yours, asking for your help, your grace. My life is yours. My heart is yours. Would you speak to me about your love and how you see me? I need your help, your revelation. I am your Bride. You are my Bridegroom. Help me to more fully understand and embrace that. Jesus, I give you access to all of my heart. I invite you into every part. Come, Holy Spirit, have your way . . . that I might love you, God, more deeply and truly with all of my heart, soul, mind, and strength. In Jesus' name I pray. Amen.

Windows to Your Heart

We believe that God has set in every human heart the longing for romance. And that he speaks to us about the Great Romance in so many ways—in songs, in stories, of course in Scripture, and also through the beauty of the earth. In this chapter we suggested that you go back to the movies that you love. Think of one of the most romantic scenes you can remember, one that made you sigh. Jack with Rose on the bow of the Titanic, his arms around her waist, their first kiss. Wallace speaking in French to Muron, then in Italian: "Not as beautiful as you." Aragorn standing with Arwen in the moonlight on the bridge in Rivendell declaring their love. Edward returning for Eleanor in Sense and Sensibility and Professor Behr returning for Jo at the end of *Little Women.*

Now, put yourself in the scene as the Beauty and Jesus as the Lover.

Or perhaps you have a favorite love song. Listen to it again, as Jesus singing to you. And may we recommend "All I ask of You" from Phantom of the Opera? Listen to it as God's love song to you. Breathtaking.

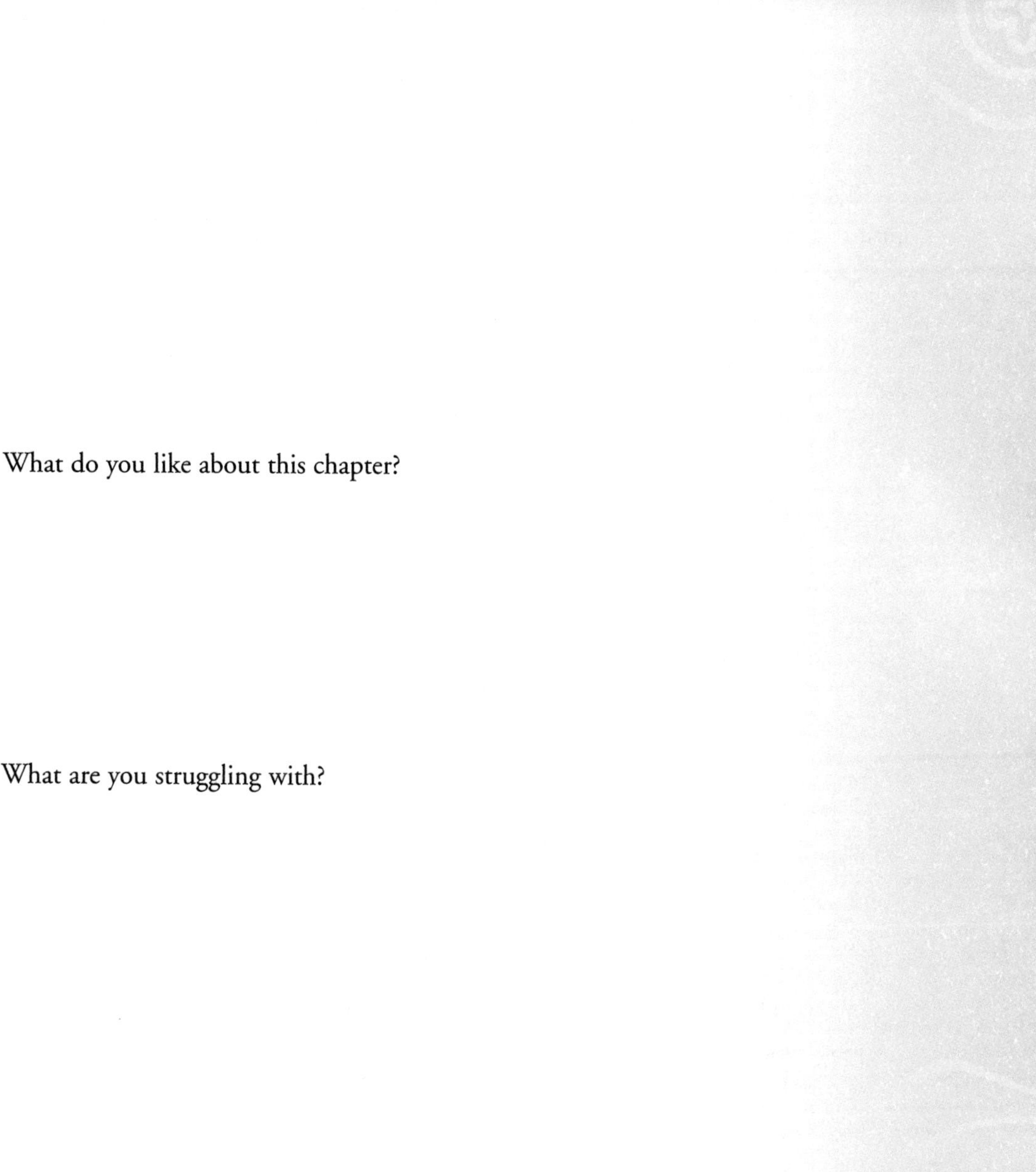

Now, go back over the chapter, skimming the pages. What does it evoke in your heart? What is your response to this chapter?

What do you like about this chapter?

What are you struggling with?

What, if anything, presented in this chapter are you having a hard time believing?

Take a few minutes now and just tell God how wonderful he is. Ask his help to turn your attention onto him. Write a love letter to him. (He will really like it!)

Longing for Romance

We opened this chapter in the companion book with me sharing the story of a walk on a starlit night, one of my first experiences of God's intimate love.

> This wild God of mine, who knows my every thought and intention, who sees my every failure and sin, loves me. Not in a religious way, not in the way we usually translate when we hear, "God loves us." Which usually sounds like "because he has to" or meaning "he tolerates you." No. He loves me as a Lover loves. Whoa.

Is this a new thought to you? A new category to think in? What do you think of it? What is your heart's response?

A woman becomes beautiful when she knows she's loved. We've seen this many times—you probably have, too. Cut off from love, rejected, no one pursuing her, something in a woman wilts like a flower no one waters anymore. She withers into resignation, duty, and shame. The radiance of her countenance goes out, as if a light has been turned off. But this same woman, who everyone thought was rather plain and unengaging, becomes lovely and inviting when she is *pursued.* Her heart begins to come alive, come to the surface, and her countenance becomes radiant. We wonder, "Where has she been all these years? Why—she really is captivating." Think of Fran in *Strictly Ballroom,* or Tulah in *My Big Fat Greek Wedding.* Remember Lottie in *Enchanted April,* Adrian in *Rocky,* or Danielle in *Ever After.* Their beauty was always there. What happened was merely the power of romance *releasing* their true beauty, awakening their hearts. They came alive.

Have you ever been in love? How did you feel? How did you feel about yourself?

As women we long to be loved in a certain way, a way unique to our femininity. We long for romance. We are wired for it; it's what makes our hearts come alive. You know that. Somewhere, down deep inside, you know this. But what you might never have known is this . . .

Romance doesn't need to wait for a man. God longs to bring this into your life himself.

God wants you to move beyond the childlike "Jesus loves me, this I know, for the Bible tells me so." He wants to heal us through his love to become mature women who actually know him. He wants us to experience verses like, "Therefore I am now going to allure her; I will lead her into the desert and speak tenderly to her" (Hos. 2:14 NKJV). And "You have stolen my heart, my sister, my bride" (Song 4:9 NKJV). Our hearts are desperate for this.

Dream a little. What would it be like to experience for yourself that the truest thing about God's heart toward yours is not disappointment or disapproval but *deep, fiery, passionate love*? (This is, after all, what a woman was made for.) What would change in your life?

What would alter in the way you perceive yourself?

What would change in the way you perceive God?

Faithful obedience to God is vital, but it is not all God draws us to. It is not sufficient for our healing, no more than doing the laundry is sufficient for a marriage. And it will not be enough in the long run to carry us through.

What do we need to live the life God has called us to—or better, *invited* us to live?

Lifting the Veil

In this chapter I said, "The root of all holiness is Romance."

My hunch is that many of you have never heard that before. So let me explain. Jesus said "If you love Me, keep My commandments" (John 14:15 NKJV). By this he didn't mean, "Prove it. Prove you love me by obeying the Law." No, what he was describing was the beauty of a heart in love with him. "The natural result of your heart in love with me will be to keep my commands. You'll want to. Any other life will seem dull and hollow and unappealing."

When you love someone, you want to please them. You want to do the things they want to do. The same holds true in your walk with God.

Does that begin to make sense to you—that romance with God is the root of all holiness?

God as Lover

Let's go back for a moment to the movies that you love. Think of one of the most romantic scenes you can remember, scenes that made you sigh. What are they?

Now put yourself in the scene as the Beauty and Jesus as the Lover. What does your heart do with that?

It's okay. It's quite biblical. Jesus calls himself the Bridegroom (Matt. 9:15; Matt. 25:1–10; John 3:29). Now, you'll need to take the religious drapery and sanctimonious gilding off of this. "Bridegroom" simply means fiancé. Lover. This is the most intimate of all the metaphors Jesus chose to describe his love and longing for us, and the kind of relationship he invites us into.

If you'll open your heart to the possibility, you'll find that God has been wooing you ever since you were a little girl. Yes, we said earlier that the story of your life is the story of the long and sustained assault upon your heart by the one who knows what you could be and fears you. But that is only part of the story. Every story has a villain. Every story also has a hero.

The Great Love Story the Scriptures are telling us about also reveals a Lover who longs for you. *The story of your life is also the story of the long and passionate pursuit of your heart by the One who knows you best and loves you most.*

God has written the Romance not only on our hearts but all over the world around us. What we need is for him to open our eyes, to open our ears that we might recognize his voice calling to us, see his hand wooing us in the beauty that quickens our hearts.

Pray. Ask him to.

> *Jesus, open my eyes. Reveal to me the ways that you wooed me in my youth. Show me the ways that you are wooing me now!*

What are some of your favorite songs?

Favorite memories?

What were the things that romanced your heart as a girl? Was it horses in a field? Was it the fragrance of the air after a summer rain? Was it a favorite book like *The Secret Garden*? The first snowfall of winter?

Those were all whispers from your Lover, notes sent to awaken your heart's longings. And as we journey into a true intimacy with God as women, he often brings those things back into our lives, to remind us he was there, to heal and restore things that were lost or stolen.

What would you like God to restore to you?

Opening Our Hearts to the Romancer

Every song you love, every memory you cherish, every moment that has moved you to holy tears has been given to you from the One who has been pursuing you from your first breath in order to win your heart. God's version of flowers and chocolates and candlelight dinners comes in the form of sunsets and falling stars; moonlight on lakes and cricket symphonies; warm wind, swaying trees, lush gardens, and fierce devotion.

Ask Jesus for the eyes to see how he is romancing your heart today. What are the things that take your breath away? The things that make you cry or fill your heart with longing?

Jesus, how are you romancing me now?

The romancing of your heart will be immensely personal. God knows what moves you. And he delights in revealing himself, revealing his love to those who will seek him with their whole heart. It is ok to ask him for more! Ask him to romance you this week, even today.

The Ebb and Flow

This is not to say that our lives are lived as one big romantic moment with Jesus. It is saying, however, that the Romance is the deepest thing, the foundation of our relationship with him.

All relationships ebb and flow. Yes? How would you describe your relationship with God over the past several months?

The ebbing in our experience of God is to draw out our hearts in deeper longing. In the times of emptiness, an open heart notices. When you are aware of a distance, an ebbing in your heart with God, what do you feel?

Often God allows these feelings to surface to help us go back to times when we have felt like this before. Notice also, what do you want to do and how do you handle your heart? Are you shutting down in anger? Turning to food? To others? How do you usually handle your heart when it is aching?

What is crucial is that next time, we handle our hearts differently.

We ask our Lover to come for us, and we keep our hearts open to his coming. We choose not to shut down. We let the tears come. We allow the ache to swell into a longing prayer for our God. And he comes, dear hearts. He does come. The times of intimacy—the flowing waters of love—those times then bring healing to places in our hearts which still need his touch.

Where are the places you would like him to come? To heal? To love?

Ask him to come.

What Does God Want from You?

Over the years, what have you believed God most wanted from you? Was it obedience? Service? Trust? What?

Are you beginning to grasp more deeply what it is that God wants from you? What he is after?

While reading George MacDonald several years ago, I came across an astounding thought. You've probably heard that there is in every human heart a place that God alone can fill. (Lord knows we've tried to fill it with everything else, to our utter dismay.) But what the old poet was saying was that there is also in God's heart a place that you alone can fill. "It follows that there is also a chamber in God himself, into which none can enter but the one, the individual." You. You are meant to fill a place in the heart of God no one and nothing else can fill.

He longs for you.

You are the one that overwhelms his heart with just one glance of your eyes (Song 4:9b NKJV). You are the one he sings over with delight and longs to dance with across mountain tops and ballroom floors (Zeph. 3:17). You are the one who takes his breath away by your beautiful heart that, against all odds, hopes in him. Let that be true for a moment. Let it be true of you.

Sit with that truth. Ponder it. What is your heart's response?

In order to have intimacy with you, he has gone to great lengths . . . and continues to do so. Here's how the flow goes in Hosea.

Therefore I will block her path with thornbushes;
I will wall her in so that she cannot find her way.
She will chase after her lovers but not catch them;
she will look for them but not find them.
—Hosea 2:6–7 NKJV

"In that day," declares the Lord,
"you will call me 'my husband';
you will no longer call me 'my master . . .'

I will betroth you to me forever;
I will betroth you in righteousness and justice,
in love and compassion."
—Hosea 2:16, 19 NKJV

What will we call the Lord?

Our hearts yearn to be loved intimately, personally, and yes, romantically. We are created to be the object of desire and affection of one who is totally and completely in love with us. And we are.

Do you believe this to be true for you?

You may have questions here for God. Go ahead and ask him.

Adoring Hearts

An intimate relationship with Jesus is not only for other women, for women who seem to have their acts together, who appear godly, and whose nails are nicely shaped. It is for each and every one of us. God wants intimacy with you. In order to have it, you, too, must offer it to him.

As Jesus and his disciples were on their way, he came to a village where a woman named Martha opened her home to him. She had a sister called Mary, who sat at the Lord's feet listening to what he said. But Martha was distracted by all the preparations that had to be made. She came to him and asked, "Lord, don't you care that my sister has left me to do the work by myself? Tell her to help me!"

"Martha, Martha," the Lord answered, "you are worried and upset about many things, but only one thing is needed. Mary has chosen what is better, and it will not be taken away from her."

—Luke 10:38–42 NKJV

What is the one thing that is needed?

Lifting the Veil

You've probably heard a lot about "worship" over the years, if you've spent any time in church. But what is worship? Is it singing hymns?

Worship is what we give our hearts away to in return for a promise of life.

It's that simple. It's an issue of the heart. Now, some worship fashion, others worship a boyfriend or husband. We really are limitless in what we will give our hearts away to.

What have you given your heart away to?

Jesus is the only One worthy of our heart's devotion. Mary recognized who Jesus was—the Source of all Life. Love Incarnate. She did what you and I hope we, too, would have done. She dropped everything and sat at his feet, fixing the gaze of her eyes and the gaze of her heart upon him.

We can do that still! We can do it today! Now. Take a few minutes and turn your heart towards Jesus. Tell him why he is worthy of your love.

Martha is a picture of the distracted bride. There is so much to be done. What is distracting you? Make a list.

Is it possible that you are doing more than God desires you to be doing?

Why not ask him? People have a tendency to put extra "yokes" on others. But Jesus said that his yoke is easy and his burden light. Ask him if there are some things he would like you to give up and stop doing in order to make more room in your life for rest . . . for him. Write down what you think it might be.

Now for one of the most beautiful mysteries of the feminine heart: women minister something to the heart of God that men do not. A tenderness, a mercy, an intimacy. There is only one time that Jesus says that what a person did to him, did for him, was *beautiful.* What was it?

Women hold a special place in the heart of God. A woman's worship brings Jesus immense pleasure and a deep ministry. You can minister to the heart of God. You impact Him. You matter.

How does that make you feel?

God is waiting. He longs for you. Offer your heart to him.

Cultivating Intimacy

Intimacy with Jesus takes cultivating. Relationships grow over time. To become intentional about cultivating a heart of worship, a heart of devoted adoration is a beautiful thing. Do you want this? If so, what will you have to let go of in order to make room for private worship in your life?

If no, what are you afraid of?

To pursue intimacy with Christ, you will have to fight for it. You'll need to fight busyness (Martha's addiction). You'll need to fight accusations. You'll need to fight the Thief that would steal your Lover's gifts to you outright. That's okay. There is a fierceness in women that was given to us for a purpose. Getting time with your Lover is worth whatever it costs.

What will *you* have to fight?

Ask his help in making you desperately hungry for him.

Ask his help in creating the time and space you need to draw close to him.

Ask him to come, to reveal himself to you as the Lover that he is.

Go get some worship music that moves you. Not music you'd do aerobics to, but music that speaks of an intimacy with Christ. Music that draws out your heart. (One of my current favorite artists is Darrell Evans. I love his "Let the River Flow" and "Freedom" CDs.)

Get in a private place. Unplug the phone. Limit the distractions. Let the ones that flow through your mind play themselves out. Write them down, what you need to do, clean, buy, make—then set them aside.

Bring your Bible and a journal to write down what you hear God say in the depths of your heart. Kneel, sit, or lie down and ask the Holy Spirit to come and help you worship Jesus. Start by telling Jesus how wonderful he is. Remember when he took care of that hard situation? Or that time he answered your prayers for financial help? Recall the times he spoke to you in your loneliness or need. Thank him for being so faithful. Stay. Linger. Worship. Let the music help usher your heart into God.

Go ahead. Find time this week to give it a try. Give yourself at least half an hour. Ask Jesus to come, to reveal himself to your heart.

Remember, this is something we grow in. We cultivate intimacy. We practice the presence of God.

To be spiritual is to be in a Romance with God. What is your heart's response now to that truth?

Sigh. Breathe. Christianity is even better than you thought. *Jesus* is better than you thought! And as we grow in knowing him, he just continues to get more so. Come. Sit at his feet.

One thing I ask of the LORD,
this is what I seek;
that I may dwell in the house of the LORD
all the days of my life,
to gaze upon the beauty of the LORD
and to seek him in his temple
—PSALM 27:4 NKJV

CHAPTER EIGHT

Beauty to Unveil

Beauty is dangerous.
—Gerard Manley Hopkins

Beauty will save the world.
—Fyodor Dostoyevsky

Show me your face, let me hear your voice;
For your voice is sweet and your face is lovely.
—Song of Songs 2:14 NKJV

This chapter is about beauty. The subject of beauty is incredibly difficult to put words to. This chapter is devoted to begin to unveil what beauty is and its redemptive, life-giving place in our world. Beauty has been the source of much anguish and grief and longing. And you possess it, simply by being a woman. *For beauty is the essence of femininity.*

Before we journey further, let's pray and ask Jesus to come, help us.

> *Dear Jesus, I love you. I need you. I come before you now, once again, as yours, asking for your help, your grace. My life is yours. My heart is yours. Would you please come and shine your light into the depths of my heart that I might understand myself better and come to know your healing and your presence more deeply. Reveal my beauty to me, Lord, as you*

reveal yours. Jesus, I give you access to all of my heart. I invite you into every part. Come, Holy Spirit, have your way . . . that I might love you, God, more deeply and truly with all of my heart, soul, mind, and strength. In Jesus' name I pray. Amen.

Windows to Your Heart

We've recommended a favorite movie of ours now for years—*Strictly Ballroom.* It's a quirky Australian movie that turns out to be simply amazing—the story of a young woman's courage to live from her heart, and how her beauty emerges and calls forth the strength of a man. Together, their redemption brings freedom to many.

Now, go back over the chapter, skimming the pages. What does it evoke in your heart?

What do you like about this chapter? What moves you?

What do you not like about it? What are you struggling with?

What, if anything, presented in this chapter are you having a hard time believing?

The Strength of a Man

The essence of a man is Strength. A man is meant to be the incarnation—our experience in human form—of our Warrior God. A God who comes through for us.

> *Who is this coming from Edom,*
> *from Bozrah, with his garments stained crimson?*
> *Who is this, robed in splendor,*
> *striding forward in the greatness of his strength?*
> *"It is I, speaking in righteousness,*
> *mighty to save."*
>
> —Isaiah 63:1 NKJV

Isn't this what makes our hearts beat more quickly, our knees weak when we watch Daniel Day Lewis in *The Last of the Mohicans* or William Wallace in *Braveheart*, Aragorn in *The Lord of the Rings* or Harrison Ford in nearly any of his movies?

Isn't that what we, as women, long to experience from our man, and from the men in our lives?

How have you experienced masculine strength in good ways, personally?

Near the beginning of this chapter, I shared the story of John interceding for me; intervening on my behalf in prayer and the breakthrough it brought to my heart. Have you ever had a man step in spiritually on your behalf? How?

Have you ever had a man step in physically on your behalf? How?

Strength is what the world longs to experience from a man. Do you understand that by strength we don't mean big muscles? So then you can see that when we speak about the essence of a woman—her beauty—we don't mean "the perfect figure." The beauty of a woman is first a soulish beauty.

The Essence of a Woman

The essence of a woman is Beauty. She is meant to be the incarnation—our experience in human form—of a Captivating God. A God who invites us.

> *"Come, all you who are thirsty, come to the waters . . .*
> *Listen, listen to me, and eat what is good,*
> *and your soul will delight in the richest of fare."*
>
> —Isaiah 55:1–2 NKJV

Beauty is what the world longs to experience from a woman. We know that. Somewhere down deep, we know it to be true. Most of our shame comes from this knowing and feeling that we have failed here. So listen to this: beauty is an essence that dwells in every woman. It was given to her by God. It was given to you.

Do you believe that?

Have you ever thought or said, "That was a beautiful thing she did"?

Do you see and experience beauty in other women? How?

What is beautiful to you?

In art?

In nature?

In music?

In others?

All beauty speaks of God. For God is nothing if not Beautiful.

Lifting the Veil

Beauty is powerful. (You might want to read that passage in chapter two again.) Beauty may be the most powerful thing on earth. Beauty speaks. Beauty invites. Beauty nourishes. Beauty comforts. Beauty inspires. Beauty is transcendent. Beauty draws us to God.

Simone Weil wrote, "The beauty of the world is almost the only way by which we can allow God to penetrate us . . . Beauty captivates the senses in order to obtain permission to pass straight through to the soul . . . The soul's inclination to love beauty is the trap God most frequently uses in order to win it."

God has given this Beauty to Eve, to every woman. Beauty is core to a woman—who she is and what she longs to be—and one of the most glorious ways we bear the image of God in a broken and often ugly world.

How do you bring beauty to your world?

How do you long to?

In your relationships?

Where you live?

Where you work?

Beauty Flows from a Heart at Rest

Beauty is the most essential and, yes, the most misunderstood of all the feminine qualities. We want you to hear clearly that it is an essence every woman carries from the moment of her creation. The only things standing in the way of our beauty are our doubts and fears and the hiding and striving we fall to as a result.

Think of a friend who you find truly lovely. What is it about her that is so lovely?

How does she make you feel when you are with her?

Lifting the Veil

Has anyone ever told you that you are beautiful?

If yes, did you believe them?

Regardless if someone has told you that you are beautiful or not, this is something every woman wonders and needs an answer to. Who is qualified to speak to your heart of the beauty found there? Remember? God. Keep asking him.

We tell the story of two women. One young, fit, physically attractive and the other much older. And it was the older woman, June, who captivated with her beauty. What was the difference between these two women?

A woman is most beautiful when she is at rest.

The choice a woman makes is not to conjure beauty but to let her defenses down. To choose to set aside her normal means of survival and just let her heart show up. Beauty comes with it.

What do you think of that?

Have you seen it? The softness that comes over a woman after she has shed vulnerable tears? The true loveliness that shines out of a woman when she is freely enjoying herself?

Your beauty should not come from outward adornment, such as braided hair and the wearing of gold jewelry and fine clothes. Instead, it should be that of your inner self, the unfading beauty of a gentle and quiet spirit. . . .

—1 PETER 3:3–4 NKJV

A young friend of mine is an eleventh grader at a well respected private Christian school. Recently, her Bible teacher quoted this Scripture and began to teach that God likes women to be quiet, a bit timid, introverted. He told his class that the Bible doesn't speak highly of women who are loud. (How highly does it speak of men who are loud?) How have *you* understood this Scripture?

Let's unpack it a little. First, Peter is not saying that we shouldn't enjoy wearing pretty things. What he's trying to say is that true beauty comes from the inner part of us: our hearts. A heart at rest. To have a gentle and quiet spirit is to have *a heart of faith*; a heart that trusts in God, a spirit that has been quieted by his love and filled with his peace, not a heart that is striving and restless. How does God quiet our hearts?

"He will quiet you with his love"

—ZEPHANIAH 3:17 NKJV

A woman in her glory, a woman of beauty, is a woman who is not striving to become beautiful or worthy or enough. She knows in her quiet center where God dwells that he finds her beautiful, has deemed her worthy, and in him, she is enough.

This is why we must keep asking Jesus to show us our beauty. Ask him what he thinks of you as a woman. His words to us let us rest and unveil our beauty.

Where has God been faithful to you? How have you known his love, mercy, and kindness?

What is the BEST possible thing God could say to you?

What would be the most wonderful thing God would want with you? From you?

Ask him. How do you see me as a woman? And keep asking. Wait for his answer. When it comes, write it down. Hold on to it. It will be better than you hoped.

Lifting the Veil

The hardest part of asking God what he sees in you as a woman, asking him to answer your deepest questions about your beauty is this: Believing what he says. Because he will speak, dear friends, and what he will say will be so very close to what your heart has wanted to hear all these years, you'll think you're making it up.

And that is how we trust him. We accept what he has to say. We let it be true.

So, what is God saying to you? If you have yet to hear from him, what do you hope he will say?

Beauty Is Inviting

Beauty beckons us. Beauty invites us. Come; explore; immerse yourself. God—Beauty himself—invites us to know him. "Taste and see that the LORD is good" (Ps. 34:8 NKJV). He delights in alluring us, and in revealing himself to those who wholeheartedly seek him. He wants to be known, to be explored. And a woman does, too.

Have you ever had the experience of wanting to get closer to something beautiful? Maybe even become a part of it?

The unveiled beauty of a woman entices and invites. The heart of the woman determines what it is she is inviting others to—to life or to death.

Proverbs speaks about two different women, two archetypes. One is Lady Folly, the other, Lady Wisdom. How are they the same? How are they different?

The way we choose to live is the way we invite others to live. A woman who is striving invites others to strive. Have you ever experienced this? What's it like to be around a striving woman? What do you feel the pressure to do? And, what *don't* you feel free to do?

By contrast, a woman whose heart is at rest invites others to rest, too. Have you experienced that? What's it like to be around a restful woman? What do you feel the freedom to do?

A woman who is hiding invites others to do the same. "Don't be vulnerable. Hide yourself." A woman who makes herself vulnerable and available for intimacy invites others to do the same. A woman who is controlling cannot invite others to rest, to be known. They will feel controlled in her presence. It won't feel safe there.

What do you most feel around the women in your life?

What are *you* most often inviting others to do? Do you have the courage to ask them?

What do you *want* to invite others to?

A woman whose heart has been quieted by the Love of God, invites others to LIFE when she unveils her beauty. Redeemed Eve is the incarnation of the heart of God for intimacy. She says to the world, through her invitation to relationship, you are wanted here. We want to know you. Come in. Share yourself. Be enjoyed. Enjoy me as I share myself.

Again, this is something that we grow in. This is where we "work out" our salvation as God works in us (Phil. 2:12–13 NKJV). As you begin to live like this, you discover the places in your heart that still need the healing touch of Jesus. That's how it goes. We don't get to stay in hiding until we are whole; Jesus invites us to live as an inviting woman now and to find our healing along the way.

What is your heart's response to this? What are you feeling?

Offering Beauty

For a woman to unveil her beauty means she is offering her heart. Not primarily her works or her usefulness (think Martha in the kitchen), but offering her presence.

What does that mean to you?

> *Beauty overwhelms us, enchants us, fascinates us, and calls us.*
>
> —Fr. Andrew Greeley

Have you ever been talking with someone, or having coffee, or at a party, and the person is with you but they don't *really* feel *with* you? The person seems distracted or uninterested? How did that make you feel?

Have you had a friend ask you "How are you?" but not really want to know your answer? Of course you have. Like me, you've probably asked people how they are as well, but not had the time or the inclination to really hear their response. On the other hand, have you sat with a friend and had their undivided attention and interest? Have you had others ask you "How are you doing?" and really want to know . . . and they're willing to wait for your answer? How did that feel?

That is offering the gift of *presence*. Presence is being present in every way, physically, emotionally, mentally. It means listening to someone wholeheartedly, engaged, without thinking of what you have to do next or what you will say next. It can be hard to slow down our minds, and really be there with people, for people. But that is what we need from others. And that is what others need from us. When we offer our unguarded presence, we live like Jesus. And we invite others to do the same.

Windows to Your Heart

"I believe in being fully present," Morrie said. "That means you should be *with* the person you're with. When I'm talking to you now, Mitch, I try to keep focused only on what is going on between us. I am not thinking about something we said last week. I am not thinking about what's coming up this Friday; I am talking to you. I am thinking about you" *(Tuesdays with Morrie).*

Beauty offers mercy. A kind word. A gentle response. A woman who is full of tender mercy and soft vulnerability is a powerful and lovely woman. I struggle with offering mercy to my children when they are irritating me. And that irritation can have absolutely nothing to do with their behavior. Do you struggle with offering mercy, kindness, and patience to anyone? Who?

Can you think of a recent instance where you reacted or acted in perhaps controlling ways? What would it have been like to have responded differently? Imagine a different scenario.

Ask God to help you next time . . . to help you offer mercy, light laughter, kindness. Pay attention to how it goes.

Beauty isn't demanding. It speaks from desire. To offer your heart is to offer your *desire*, instead of your demand.

Of Course It Feels Risky

The scariest thing for a man is to offer his strength in situations where he doesn't know if it will make any difference. Or worse, that he will fail.

For a man, if he fears intimacy, then offering strength means offering intimacy. If he fears failing in his career, offering his strength means taking a promotion or accepting a new and risky project. If he fears standing up for his children against an angry school principal, then standing up for them is what he must do. If he fears committing to the woman he's been dating for five years, then offering strength is buying her a ring. If he fears initiating sex with his wife, then offering strength means initiating sexual intimacy.

Do you understand that now to be true? Have you seen it played out?

In the same way, the scariest thing for women is to offer our beauty into situations where we don't know if it will make any difference. Or worse, that we will be rejected. For our Question is, *Am I lovely?* And to be rejected is to hear a resounding, No. A woman doesn't want to offer her beauty unless she is guaranteed that it will be well received. But life offers no such guarantees. We, too, must take risks.

What is the scariest thing for you to offer? When?

If you are married, imagine that your husband comes home with a serious expression on his face and asks you to come, sit down, he wants to talk with you privately. What would you feel? What would you want to do?

(This happens in our marriage, and honestly, when it does I feel terrified. But what I do now is review in my spirit the truth that God loves me. I am *His.* I am safe, secure in him. Even if I am failing John in some huge way, I am okay. I quiet my spirit and open my heart up to hear from him.)

A few verses after Peter talks about a quiet heart, he gives us what might be the secret to releasing a woman's heart and her beauty:

Do not give way to fear.
—1 PETER 3: 6 NKJV

Isn't that why we hide, why we strive, why we control, why we do anything but offer beauty? We are afraid. We have given way to fear. Just think about your life—why you do the things you do. Have you asked yourself how much you are motivated by fear?

Ask yourself now, how much?

That is why God says to us, "*In repentance and rest is your salvation, in quietness and trust is your strength*" (Is. 30:15 NKJV). In repentance and rest.

God invites us, urges us to repent from our self-protective strategies. And to rest in his love for us, to not give way to fear, but to trust him.

You have now seen some of the ways that you are hiding. Do you also see that you are hiding because you are afraid? Of what?

We can't wait until we feel safe to love and invite. In fact, if you feel a little scared, then you're probably on the right path. Of course it's scary. It's vulnerable. It's naked. God calls us to stop hiding, to stop dominating, to trust him, and to offer our true selves. He wants us to bring to bear the weight of our lives and all that he has given to us, worked into us, and offer it to our world. To entice, allure, and invite others to Jesus by reflecting his glory in our lives.

What is God calling you to risk?

What—and *with whom*—is he calling you to offer? How?

What will it require from you? More faith in him? More trust? More healing of your heart? Sounds like the right track.

Lifting the Veil

Sadly, there will be times when our offer of our true hearts is not received well. Jesus offered like no other, and many rejected him. In those moments or seasons when that happens to us, God's invitation to us is to bring our sorrow to him. Not to shut down with, I'll never try that again. But to keep our hearts open and alive and to find our heart's refuge and healing in his love.

Letting Our Hearts Be Deepened

To possess true beauty, we must be willing to suffer. I don't like that. Just writing it down makes my heart shrink back. Yet, if Christ himself was perfected through his sufferings, why would I believe God would not do the same with me? With you?

Living in true beauty can require much waiting, much time, much tenacity of spirit. We must constantly direct our gazes toward the face of God, even in the presence of longing and sorrow. It is in the waiting that our hearts are enlarged. The waiting does not diminish us. A woman pregnant with child is enlarged in her waiting and so are our hearts. God does not always rescue us out of a painful season. You know that he does not always give to us what we so desperately want when we want it. He is after something much more valuable than our happiness. Much more substantive than our health. He is restoring and growing in us an eternal weight of glory. And sometimes . . . it hurts.

Have you known this to be true? What was a recent (or is a current) very difficult season for you? What was/is happening?

What went on (or is going on) in your relationship with God? In your faith?

I told you about sitting on the park bench with my mother, enjoying the beauty together during what was the last few days of her life and how knowing the parting that was soon to come did not diminish our enjoyment of the beauty, but rather, heightened it. Have you ever had a similar experience? (Perhaps even the last day of a vacation in a beautiful spot?) When, where? How did you feel?

A heart awakened to its sorrow is more aware, more present, more alive. To all of the facets of life.

Cultivating Beauty

Every woman possesses a captivating beauty. *Every woman.* But for most of us it has been long buried, wounded, and captive. It takes time for it to emerge into wholeness. It needs to be cultivated, restored, set free.

Life is harsh on a woman's heart. It has been hard on your heart. The assault on our beauty is real. But Jesus is urging us now to care for ourselves, watch over our hearts (Prov. 4:23). The world needs your beauty. That is why you are here. Your heart and your beauty are something to be treasured and nourished.

What are some ways you can nourish your heart?

What refreshes you?

Where do you feel closest to God?

What do you really enjoy?

If you had a whole day that you could do anything you wanted, what would the day look like? Where would you be? Would you be alone or with someone? Who? Dream a little.

Our hearts need to feed on beauty to sustain them. We need times of solitude and silence. We need times of refreshment and laughter and rest. We need to listen to the voice of God in our hearts as he tells us what we need and then go do that! He knows us well. He knows what would be best for us. And, by the way, God really likes to have fun. Often what he will tell us we need to do is something that we really enjoy.

Ask him if he would like to make your dream day happen. Ask him for it. (Or to happen really close to what our dream is.) Go ahead.

The Holy Spirit is our guide, our counselor, our comforter, our Great Friend, and he will lead us. Abiding in Christ means attending to the voice of God within, nourishing our own hearts and nourishing our relationship with him. Over time.

And guess what! Contrary to what the world claims, Beauty does not diminish with time; Beauty deepens and increases. *True beauty comes from a depth of soul that can only be attained through living many years well.* God grows it in us.

As we gaze on Jesus, as we behold his goodness, and his glory, we are changed into his likeness, the most beautiful Person of all.

They looked to Him and were radiant.
—PSALM 34:5 NKJV

What is your response to that?

We have all heard it said that a woman is most beautiful when she is in love. Have you seen that to be true?

When a woman knows that she is loved and loved deeply, she has had her heart's deepest questions answered: "Am I lovely? Am I worth fighting for? Have I been and will I continue to be romanced?" When these questions are answered, "Yes," a restful, quiet spirit settles in a woman's heart. *And every woman can have these questions answered,* "Yes."

Ask God. Does he find you lovely? Does he think you are worth fighting for?

When we are at rest in the knowledge that our God *really* loves us, we can offer our hearts to others and invite them to Life.

Faith, Hope, and Love

Unveiling our beauty really just means unveiling our feminine hearts. It's scary, for sure. That is why it is our greatest expression of faith, hope, and love. Our focus shifts from self-protection to the hearts of others.

How will offering and unveiling your heart require you to live by faith?

How will it require you to hope in God?

How will it cause you to love others sincerely?

When we offer our Beauty, we are living a life of love so that others' hearts might come alive, be healed, and grow in knowing God. And that is a noble, worthy life to live.

Take a few moments now and express your heart's desire to God.

CHAPTER NINE

Arousing Adam

Are you strong enough to be my man?
—Sheryl Crow

Come away, my lover,
and be like a gazelle
or like a young stag
on the spice-laden mountains.
—Song of Songs 8:14 NKJV

When it comes to the subject of loving a man—any of the men in your life—we need far more than a chapter. A book would barely feel sufficient. The issues are often murky, and things can get really muddy as time goes by. But we cannot pass over this subject, either. It's far too important; too many questions linger here for most women. So we will try and lay out in this chapter the deeper issues and trust the Holy Spirit to help you with the application.

Everything we said about unveiling beauty, about how a woman invites and offers—this is so much more true when it comes to loving Adam. *True femininity calls forth true masculinity.* We awaken it, arouse it in a way that nothing else on earth even comes close to.

Let's ask Jesus to help us go deeper into understanding men and how best to call forth their true masculinity.

Dear Jesus, I love you. I need you. I come before you now, once again, as yours, your woman, asking for your help, your grace. My life is yours. My heart is yours. Would you please come and shine your light into the mystery of masculinity and femininity that I might better understand myself as well as the men in my life? Help me to see, to understand, to repent, to forgive, and to become. Jesus, I give you access to all of me, every part. Come, Holy Spirit, have your way . . . that I might love you, God, more deeply and truly with all of my heart, soul, mind, and strength. And that I might truly love others. In Jesus' name I pray. Amen.

Windows to Your Heart

In the book's companion chapter John and I described several women from a movie we love called *Enchanted April.* Get a few friends together and watch it. Talk about what you see. Not only do we think you'll enjoy the movie and its theme of redemption through love, you might also find it a really helpful glimpse into the various ways fallen Eve is played out in our world—and what it looks like for her to become an alluring woman.

Now, go back over the chapter, skimming the pages. What strikes you? What does it evoke in your heart?

What do you like about this chapter?

What do you not like about it? What are you struggling with?

What does reading it make you want to *do*?

What changes do you want to make in your relationships with men?

What does John say are the two messages a man needs to hear from his wife?

Adam's Wound

If you'll watch little boys for any length of time, you'll see how deeply the Hero is written on their hearts. Their games are filled with battle and courage and a testing. Who's brave enough to jump out the second story window onto the trampoline?

What crazy things have your sons, your brothers, your girlfriend's sons done to test themselves?

When boys become teenagers, they take on an air of independence and bravado that can really drive moms nuts. It looks arrogant and defiant, but what it really is is their masculine strength emerging in an awkward stage.

Have you seen this in the young men around you? (The current fad here among young men is to wear their jeans really low, on or below their hips with their boxers showing. They look utterly ridiculous, but they think they look really cool.)

In all of this, can you see their Question: Do I have what it takes? Am I the real deal? Am I a man?

A man's deepest wounds come from the way his Question was answered in his youth. Just like yours. Every man is wounded. As he was growing up, he looked to his father to answer his Question. The result was often devastating.

Does this help shine light on the men in your lives?

In the case of violent fathers, the wound is given directly. The answer to his Question is given painfully, filling him with uncertainty and doubt. In the case of passive fathers, the wound is given indirectly. The father's silence leaves a vacuum for fear and doubt to fill.

Adam's sin and Adam's woundedness come together to result in the passivity or the drivenness you find in so many men. Why won't he talk to me? Why won't he commit? Why is he so angry? Why is he violent? You won't begin to understand a man until you understand his Question, his wound, and how Adam also fell. His search for validation is the driving force of his life.

Think of the men you are closest to. How do you think their Question was answered?

Can *you* answer it?

As much as you'd like to, you can only speak to it. You can't answer a man's deepest question. Only masculinity can bestow masculinity.

Standing in Love's Way

In *Wild at Heart* I warned men that the greatest obstacle to loving a woman was this: too many men take their Question to Eve. They look to her for the validation of their souls. Haven't you felt it?

It happens usually around adolescence, this fatal shift. The father has been silent or violent; his chance to redeem his son is nearly gone. The next window that opens in a boy's journey is his sexuality. Suddenly, he is aware of Eve. She looks like life itself to him. She looks like the answer to his Question.

It's a fatal shift. So much of the pornography addiction for men comes from this. It's not about sex—it's about validation. She makes him feel like a man. She offers him her beauty, and it makes him feel strong.

So many men struggle with pornography. Their women usually feel that it is because he finds her lacking. It is not true. It is about a man trying to get his masculinity validated in a way that requires nothing of him.

How do you respond to reading this?

John has tried in every way to help men understand that no woman can tell them who they are as a man. Masculinity is bestowed by masculinity. It cannot come from any other source. Yes—a woman can offer a man so much. She can be his *ezer*, his companion, his inspiration. But she cannot be the validation of his soul. Men have got to take their Question to God, to their Father in heaven. Only he knows who we truly are. Only he can pronounce the verdict on us. A man goes to Eve to offer his strength. He does not go to her to get it.

Now, the same holds true for you, Eve. You cannot take your Question to Adam. You cannot look to him for the validation of your soul.

Do you remember looking to boys for your validation as a teenage girl? As a young woman?

In what ways are you looking to Adam to answer your heart's Question these days?

Taking our Question to Adam is a deadly shift. No man can tell you who you are as a woman. No man is the verdict on your soul. Dear sister, have you lost yourself in this search?

Now yes, in a loving relationship, we are meant to offer to one another our strength and beauty. But our core validation, our primary validation has to come from God. And until it does, until we look to him for the healing of our souls, our relationships are really hurt by this looking-to-each-other for something only God can give. Ask Jesus to show you what you've been doing with your Question and how you've related to Adam. Only then can we talk about loving men.

How Does a Woman Love a Man?

Lets start with sex.

Not because "its all men think about" (as many a cynical woman has said), but because it presents the relationship between femininity and masculinity in such a clear way. It is a beautiful and rich metaphor, a very passionate and heightened picture for a much broader reality. The question before us is, "How does a woman best love a man?" The answer is simple:

Seduce him.

What do you think of this answer?

The beauty of a woman is what arouses the strength of a man. He *wants* to play the man when a woman acts like that. You can't hold him back. He *wants* to come through. And this is crucial—don't you want him to *want* to? Not to be forced to, not because he "ought to." But because he *wants* to come through.

Isn't this what you want?

Switch positions. Who would you rather spend an evening with, the man that says, "You look beautiful tonight!" or "You're going out in *that*?" Which man generates a desire to become ever more beautiful?

Who do you want to be beautiful to these days?

Think beyond the bedroom. What are some ways that a good woman could seduce a good man? How could you, as a woman, arouse desire in a man, to play the man? To exert his masculine strength in good ways? *To grow into becoming a more godly man?*

Inviting strength, alluring strength is so much more effective than demanding strength, challenging strength. Whining never works. It diminishes the woman and deflates the man. Yet, there are times when we need to evoke from our men movement; we need to call forth their masculinity. How do we *best* do that?

The Holy, Scandalous Women of the Bible

There are five women mentioned in the genealogy of Jesus. Now, that might not strike you as a big deal, until you understand that women are never mentioned in those genealogies. It's *always* men. These are really good women. (And by not using Bathsheba's name, God is saying, that she is not such a good woman.)

What distinguishes these women? What can we learn from them? How did they live in ways that called forth strength in the men in their lives? They have different situations, different acts of obedience. Yet the common theme is this. *Courage, Cunning* and *Stunning Vulnerability.*

Go back to the book and re-read the section about Ruth.

John wrote "She can badger him: *All you do is work, work, work. Why won't you stand up and be a man?* She can whine about it: *Boaz, pleeease hurry up and marry me.* She can emasculate him: *I thought you were a real man; I guess I was wrong.* Or she can use all she is as a woman to get him to use all he's got as a man. She can arouse, inspire, energize—seduce him."

Which kind of approach would you say you tend to take with the man/men in your life?

Which kind of approach do you think he/they would prefer?

Which kind of approach do you believe will best achieve the desired results?

Ruth *aroused* Boaz to play the man. *She awakened his desire to be the Hero.* That's the point.

Emasculating Women

Women pretty much fall into one of three categories: Dominating Women, Desolate Women, or Arousing Women. The first two are what happens to Eve as a result of the Fall. The third is a woman whose femininity is being restored by God and who offers it to others.

How would you describe your mother with your father?

How would you describe yourself?

I mentioned Annie in *The Horse Whisperer* as an example of a dominating, emasculating woman. She needs nothing from her man. She has life under control. She wears the pants in the family. Her message is clear: "You are weak and untrustworthy. I am strong. Let me lead and things will go fine." The effect on a man is not good. When a woman becomes controlling and not in the least vulnerable, her seductivity is shut down. The message is "Back off—I'll handle this." Any wonder that he backs off?

So many women fear the wildness God put in their man. They are drawn to his strength and then set about taming him once they've "caught" him. "I don't want you riding a motorcycle anymore. I don't want you hanging around your friends so much. Why do you need to go off on all those adventures?" Women who make their husbands pee sitting down.

Have you seen that done? Under the guise of, "I need you around, so be safe or available or committed"? Have you done it yourself?

What was the effect on the man?

Emasculating women send a clear message: "I don't need you. I refuse to be vulnerable and inviting. You have nothing to offer me."

Does this make sense to you? How can you let your man know you need him? How can you be more vulnerable and inviting?

Lifting the Veil

Okay. Here's a piece of daring advice. Ask him. Ask him what you are like to be with as a woman. Have him read this chapter (it might get him to read the whole book!) and then ask him what kind of woman you've been like to live with. I know—it sounds absolutely crazy. Too risky. But it just might open up whole new levels of intimacy, too!

Desolate Women

The third character in *Enchanted April* is Lottie. She is not harsh—just shut down from years of living with a selfish, domineering pig of a man. She looks like a whipped puppy, rushing to please him in any way, not out of love but out of fear and some weird idea of submission. She is depressed. Rose is Lottie's friend she meets at church. She is the Religious Woman. The typical Church Lady. She's actually quite beautiful, but she dresses in such a way as to hide it. Bag-shaped dresses, hair in a bun. Her heart is also shut down. She hides behind her prayers and her "good works of service." She is weary and tired.

Desolate women don't seem at first pass to be all that emasculating. They don't attack or dominate. But neither do they allure. Their message is simply, "There's nothing here for you." The lights are off; they have dimmed their radiance; no one is home. A man in her presence feels . . . uninvited. Unwanted. It's a form of rejection, emasculation, to be sure. But it's harder to point out because it's so subtle.

Can you relate—have you been like this towards your man, or men in general? Why?

Desolate women can also be those whose ache is what *defines* them. Women who will do whatever it takes to get a man. The Woman at the Well would be an example. She moves from lover to lover trying to fill the void within her. She's available—but in a clingy, desperate way. "Groveling," as one friend said, "manipulating, begging for attention." Like the character Catherine Zeta-Jones plays in *Terminal.* Their message to men is, "I need you too much. Please tell me who I am. Fill me." Men use women like this—but they do not love them. They do not feel challenged to be a Hero. Desolate women do not call the men in their lives to be Heroes.

Do you know women like this? What are they like—how do they relate to men?

Have you been like this—desperate for a man to love you, so desperate you have thrown yourself at him, been *too* vulnerable? How did it go?

> *If you would be loved, be loveable.*
>
> —OVID

AROUSING WOMEN

The beautiful story in *Enchanted April* is how each of the women actually becomes a woman indeed. Caroline softens, becoming tender and vulnerable. She no longer resents her beauty, but offers it gently, almost shyly, which for her is repentance. Lottie and Rose gain a sense of self. They become substantive, able to offer their men a real mate, not a doormat. They too become alluring; being *less* shy is repentance for them—no longer hiding but coming forward in a gentle way. The effect on the men in their lives is astounding. What severity and domineering and hiding and whining could not do, beauty does. Their men come forth as good men, repentant men. Heroes.

Okay. We are on the road to redemption, we are in the process of being restored. We are becoming the women we want to be, but we know we have often lived like Eve after the Fall. If you have been either a dominating and controlling woman, or a desolate and mousy woman—what would repentance look like for you? How can you begin to change the way you relate to your man?

How about sexually?

How about relationally, in the way you speak and relate to one another?

How about with decisions such as finances?

Arousing women are those who call forth the best in a man by offering who they are *as* a woman. Women who offer beauty, their true heart, like we described in the last chapter. Such a stark contrast is set out in the movie, *A Walk in the Clouds*. There are two women in Keanu Reeves' life. His wife pressures him, "You are not the man I want you to be." She is manipulating and demanding. Eventually she has an affair. The Hispanic woman he meets on the bus is alluring. A strong and self-confident women, she is also soft and inviting. Her message to him is, "You are an amazing man."

How can you begin to communicate this to your man: "You are an amazing man?"

However it is expressed in the uniqueness of your own femininity, arousing Adam comes down to this:

Need him. And believe in him.

That is what a man needs to hear from his woman more than anything else. I need you. I need your strength. I believe in you. You have what it takes.

What can you do to "say" this to your man?

Loving Fallen Men

Lifting the Veil

Granted, not every man is on the road to redemption. There are men out there who are not safe and good men. Some of you are married to one. All of you will encounter them. How do you love them? With great wisdom and cunning. The last three chapters in Dan Allender's book *Bold Love* are, "Loving an Evil Person; Loving a Fool; and Loving a Normal Sinner." You might find them helpful.

Also, if you are in a difficult marriage, we strongly urge you to get some outside perspective. Talk to a girlfriend about what's going on. Or see a counselor. It might be the best thing you ever do for your marriage.

How generous and lavish God is with his beauty towards us. He sends the sun each day; he sends music and laughter and so many notes to our hearts. But he also says, "You shall find me when you seek me with all your heart." That is a good way for a woman to live as well. Not defiant, not hiding, but alluring and watching to see if her man wants to come closer.

"Do not throw your pearls before swine," (Matt. 7:6) Jesus said. By this we don't think he was calling some people pigs. He was saying, "Look—be careful that you do not give something precious to someone who, at best, cannot recognize its beauty, or at worst, will trample on it." Consider your feminine heart and beauty your treasure, your pearls. A woman can test to see if a man is willing to move in a good direction by offering a *taste* of what is available with her if he does. She does not give everything in a moment. Like God does, she allures, and waits to see what he will do. We'll try to offer a few examples.

We told the story of Janice and how she played "Ruth" to her husband, a self-centered and selfish man. What did the story stir in you?

Betsy is the woman who was married to a verbally abusive man. What did her story stir in you?

Lifting the Veil

If you think you might be in an abusive situation—if your man abuses you verbally (such as yelling at you each night) or physically (such as hurting you in any way) or sexually (such as forcing you to have sex with him) we STRONGLY urge you to see a counselor. Do not be naïve—do not think "things will get better." Not without help they won't.

Single Women

It might be encouraging to point out that Mary, Rahab, Ruth, and Tamar were all single women when the story of their greatness was told. (True, Mary was engaged, but she had reason to believe it wouldn't last long when she gave her "Yes" to God.) They are such powerful reminders that this can be lived out as a single woman. They also stand in stark contrast to some of the messages of "purity" given single women today. As one young gal wrote to us, "I am afraid that I and numerous other women have interpreted womanly purity as 'completely ignore the man you are interested in until he proposes to you.'"

And why, then, *would* he propose to you?

To our single readers—what have you been taught a godly approach to young men looks like?

Of course a woman should be alluring to the man she is attracted to. A smile, a tenderness, an interest in him and his life are natural and welcome. To look your best, awaken him to your presence. Yes, you can offer beauty to him—in gently increasing amounts, as he pursues and comes closer. And yes, there are parts of you that should be held as mysteries until he fully commits, and you offer yourself to him on your wedding night. Don't offer everything, but don't offer nothing.

On a scale of one to ten, with one being nothing and ten being sleeping with a man you are not married to in order to "catch him," where would you put yourself? And why?

How much, and when? That is more than we can say in a chapter. Walk with God. Be a wise and discerning woman. Be aware of the issues that would cause you to hold back or give too much. Be aware of the issues in him that would cause him to look to you for his validation, or become paralyzed. Invite, arouse, and maintain your personal integrity.

You've traveled some ways in this journal, and looked at your wounds and the assaults you've endured, and seen some of the ways they have shaped you into the woman you are now. Can you see the way your past is shaping the way you relate to men?

There is an emotional promiscuity we've noticed among many good young men and women. The young man understands something of the journey of the heart. He wants to talk, to "share the journey." The woman is so grateful to be pursued that she opens up. They share the intimacies of their lives—their wounds, their walk with God. But he never commits. He enjoys her . . . and then leaves. And she wonders, *What did I do wrong*? She failed to see his passivity—he really did not ever commit or offer assurances that he would. Like Willouby to Marianne in *Sense and Sensibility*.

Have you seen this going on with your friends? Have you done it? What happened?

Be careful you do not offer too much of yourself to a man until you have good, solid evidence that he is a strong man willing to commit. Look at his track record with other women. Is there anything to be concerned about there? If so, bring it up. Also, does he have any close male friends—what are *they* like as men? Can he hold down a job? Is he walking with God in a real and intimate way? Is he facing the wounds of his own life, and is he also demonstrating a desire to repent of Adam's passivity and/or violence? Is he headed somewhere with his life? A lot of questions, but your heart is a treasure and we want you to offer it only to a man who is worthy and ready to handle it well.

How does the man in your life measure up on each of these questions? Be frank and honest.

Is there cause for concern?

Lifting the Veil

Your friends should like him. Whether it's a man you are dating or the man you are married to, do not ignore the opinions of people you trust. Let them be honest with you—especially before you marry someone. You might be making a mistake.

But let them be honest in their assessment of your man after marriage, too! You might have grown numb to major issues of concern, "learned to live with it." That's not love—that's survival. It might be time for some honest conversation—or counseling.

To close, woman was given to man to be his *ezer*—his *life-saver.* It's a challenging job and can only be done well by a woman who is in an intimate, holy Romance with God. He will guide us. He will teach us. God allures us to himself. He invites us to join him in alluring others to him as well.

Arousing Adam means alluring the men in your life to God. Not by demanding. Not by controlling. Not by whining. But by faith, hope and love enticing them to become ever more the man God created them to be.

And how exactly do we do that? By first becoming ever more the woman God created us to be.

What does that mean to you? What would that look like in your life today?

Let's pray.

Dear Jesus. I don't quite understand this yet. I know the addage that you catch more bees with honey than with vinegar, but how do I entice men to godliness without manipulating them? You say in your word that a godly woman can win her unbelieving husband to Christ without speaking a word but by her behaviour. I want to know that. I want to become a woman who entices the men in my life to become more yours through my behaviour, my life-giving words and my feminine heart. Teach me Lord. Please help me here. I trust you. I give you all my relationships with men and ask you to redeem them and have your way. In Jesus' name. Amen.

CHAPTER TEN

Mothers, Daughters, Sisters

Adam named his wife Eve, because she would
become the mother of all the living.
—Genesis 3:20 NKJV

How wide and sweet and wild motherhood—and sisterhood—can be.
—Rebecca Wells

We have our mother tongue, which is our native language. We have mother earth from which all growing things come and Mother Nature, the unpredictable source of typhoons and tornadoes. The mother lode is the source of riches and a "mother headache" is one that sends you to bed. The mother of all storms is fierce, and the motherland is the home we left and long for. Mother is the source of life. Mother is powerful. Mother is strong. Mother can nurture, and mother can destroy. Depending on our individual experiences, the word "mother" can evoke images of a warm, welcoming woman or turn our blood to ice.

Whether good or bad, whether redemptive or destructive, our relationships with our mothers affected us to the core of our beings, helping to shape us into the women we have become. As Dinah says in *The Red Tent*, "If you want to understand any woman you must first ask about her mother and then listen carefully."

This chapter is devoted to the holy, rocky terrain of relationships among and between women. Before we journey deeper into this realm, let's ask for God's hand to hold our hearts and guide us.

Dear Jesus, I love you. I need you. I come before you now, once again, as yours, asking for your help, your grace. My life is yours. My heart is yours. Would you please come and shine your light into the depths of my heart that I might understand myself and my relationships better and come to know your healing and your presence more deeply. Help me to remember what I need to remember. Help me to see, to understand, to repent, to forgive, and to become. Jesus, I give you access to all of my heart. I invite you into every part. Come, Holy Spirit, have your way . . . that I might love you, God, more deeply and truly with all of my heart, soul, mind, and strength. In Jesus' name I pray. Amen.

Windows to Your Heart

There are so many wonderful stories about mothers and daughters, and the friendships of women. *Little Women* is a classic for a reason. If you haven't seen the latest film version in awhile (or avoided it completely!), have another look.

Also, may we recommend two wonderful songs: "Anita's Heart" by Fernando Ortega speaks of the pain of a mother's heart; "I Am" by Jill Phillips is our favorite song about the mother-love of God.

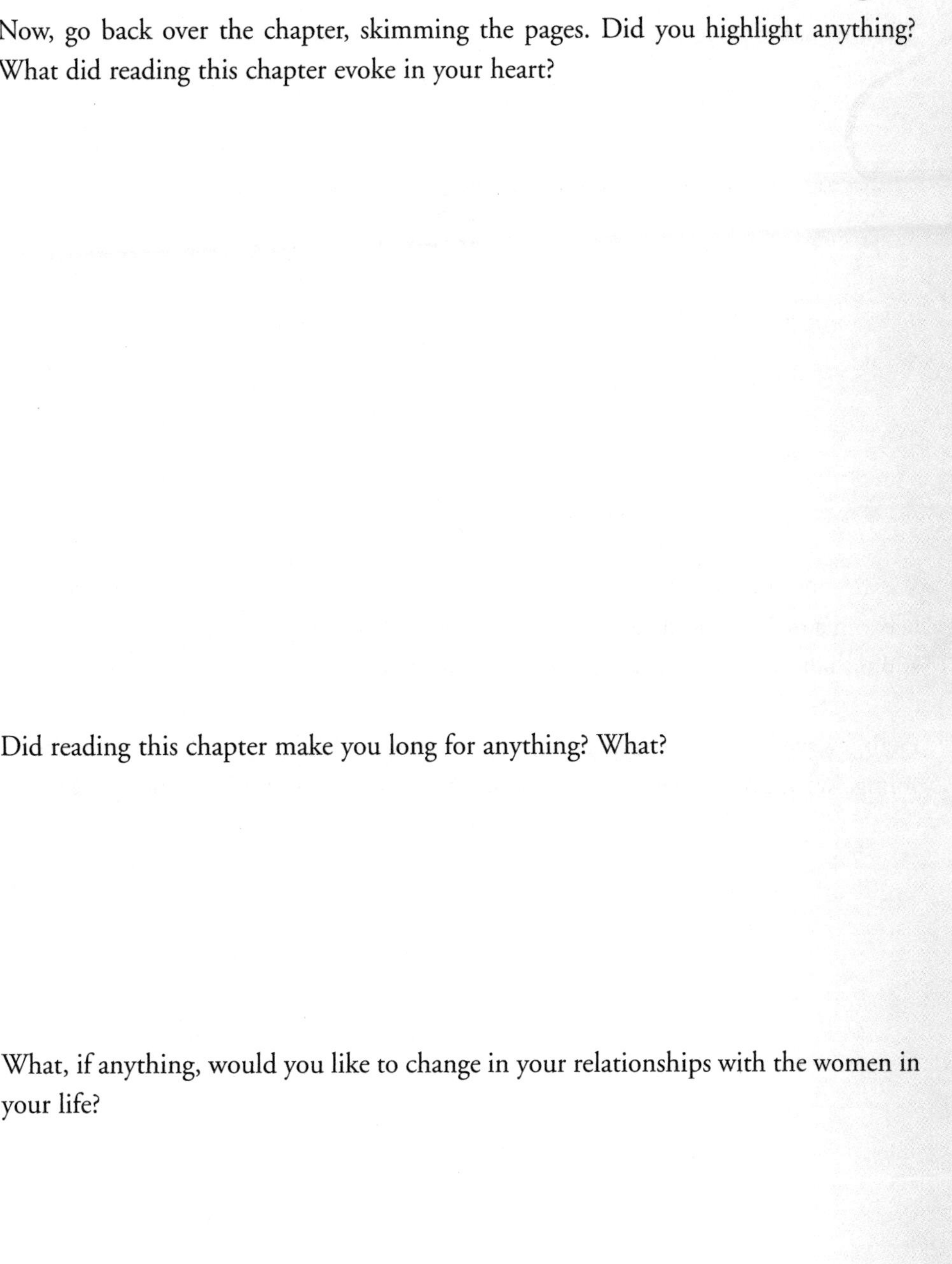

Now, go back over the chapter, skimming the pages. Did you highlight anything? What did reading this chapter evoke in your heart?

Did reading this chapter make you long for anything? What?

What, if anything, would you like to change in your relationships with the women in your life?

What would that require of you?

Our Mothers

We are not all mothers, but we all had one. Or longed for one. The relationship between a mother and daughter is a holy, tender, fierce thing fraught with land mines and umbilical cords that stretch and sometimes strangle.

Put a few words to what your relationship with your mother was like when you were young. What do you remember? Any special moments? Any painful memories?

Did your relationship with your mother change when you became an adolescent? What was it like?

Did she take you shopping? Did you have similar tastes, similar interests?

Did she know the deeper waters of your heart?

Lifting the Veil

You have probably heard it said that you cannot pass on what you do not possess. It means that a woman with very low self-esteem will be unable to pass on very high self-esteem to her daughter, even though she may want to very much. We received from our mothers some of the same issues that they struggled deeply with even though they may play out differently in our lives. Unintentionally, our brokenness gets passed down. (This is one of the greatest motivators for a woman to seek inner healing from God—so she can give to her children the best possible foundation.)

What is your relationship with your mom like these days? Would you say you are close?

Do you feel like your mother truly knows you? Wants to know you?

Many a good woman makes the desperate mistake of believing that her daughter is a reflection of herself, an extension of herself, and therefore the verdict on her as a mother, and as a woman.

If you are a mother of a daughter, do you feel this pull inside of you? Do you believe that your daughter's choices reflect on you?

Did your mother feel this way about you?

Girl's hearts flourish in homes where they are seen and invited to become ever more themselves. Parents who enjoy their daughters are giving them and the world a great gift. Mothers in particular have the opportunity to offer encouragement to their daughters by inviting them into their feminine world and by treasuring their daughter's unique beauty.

The Long Road Home

In this section of the chapter in the companion book, I shared with you some of the story of my relationship with my mom and the reconciliation and restoration that God brought to us. In reading it, what did it evoke in your heart?

Is your mother someone that you have a relationship with, or would like to?

If she is still living, how do you feel around your mother?

How do you think she feels around you?

What would you like to see change in your relationship with your mom? What needs healing and restoration?

What would that require of you?

What would the best possible relationship with your mother look like? Put some words to your heart's desire. Dream big.

Now, go ahead, and ask God for it.

THE COST

It is one thing to suffer. It is something far worse to walk alongside one you love who is suffering intensely and be unable to do anything about it. Many of you have lived this. You know.

Have you experienced this? With whom? What was happening?

A woman bleeds when she gives birth, but that is only the beginning of the bleeding. A heart enlarged by all a mother endures with and through her child's life, all a mother prays and works and hopes for on her child's behalf, bleeds, too.

If you have children, what are you aching for in their lives?

Lifting the Veil

She's praying again her daughter will land with both feet on the ground.
Nobody knows which way she'll go, or if she'll ever come around.
Maybe this time she'll finally find the pieces that have come apart,
And there'll be no more breaking, no more breaking either heart.

She carries around a photograph of her beautiful coltish girl
In a big white shirt, her head tossed back, a free spirit in this world.
You want to forget all that she's done and all she's compromised.
You can close your eyes and believe that now she's the same girl in disguise.

"Anita's Heart"—Fernando Ortega

A mother's heart is a vast and glorious thing. My mother's heart was expansive, having been enlarged by suffering and years of clinging to Jesus while being misunderstood, dismissed, and judged by those she loved most. Me included. It had cost her to love, had cost her much to mother. It always does. But she would tell you that it's worth it; that there is no other way.

Both my parents are gone now, off and away and fully alive in heaven. I tell you this story because I want you to know that redemption is possible. Healing is possible. Ask Jesus to bring it to you and yours. Then, if you can, go, call your mother. Tell her you love her.

Can you do this?

To Mother

As large as the role is that our mothers have played, the word "mother" is more powerful when used as a verb than as a noun. All women are not mothers, but all women are called to mother. To mother is to nurture, to train, to educate, to rear. In doing this, women partner with Christ in the vital mission of bringing forth life.

Who has mothered you in the course of your life? How?

Who have you mothered? How?

Mothering someone is seeing them as they really are and calling them out to be that person.

All women are called to mother. And all women are called to give birth. Women give birth to all kinds of things—to a book (it's nearly as hard as a child; believe me), to a church, or to a movement. Women give birth to ideas, to creative expressions, to ministries. We birth life in others by inviting them into deeper realms of healing, to deeper walks with God, to deeper intimacy with Jesus. A woman is not less of a woman because she is not a wife or has not physically born a child. The heart and life of a woman is much more vast than that.

What have you "given birth" to?

What would you love to give birth to?

My Sister, My Friend

All women are made in the image of God in that we bring forth life. When we enter into our world and into the lives of those we love and offer our tender and strong feminine hearts, we cannot help but mother them.

I love the way women friends have with each other. When I gather with a group of women friends, inevitably someone begins to rub someone else's back. Hair gets played with. Merciful, tender, caressing, healing touches are given.

Have you seen this? Experienced it?

The capacity of a woman's heart for meaningful relationships is vast. There is no way your husband or your children can ever provide the intimacy and relational satisfaction you need. A woman must have women friends.

Do you have girlfriends? A best friend? Who are they?

Are you satisfied with your relationship with them or do you desire more?

What do you long for in your friendships?

If you don't have a close friendship with a woman you trust and enjoy, take a few minutes now and ask God to bring her into your life. Be like the stubborn widow and *keep* asking him.

There is a fierce jealousy, a fiery devotion, and a great loyalty between women friends. Our friendships flow in the deep waters of the heart where God dwells and transformation takes place. It is here, in this holy place, that a woman can partner with God in impacting another and be impacted by another for lasting good. It is here that she can mother, nurture, encourage, and call forth Life.

Friendship is a great gift. How can you nurture, guard, and fight for your friendships?

How do you offer your heart to your friends?

How do they offer their heart to you?

Awkward Love

And let me say clearly, true friendship is *opposed.* One woman often feels less important or accused or needy or misunderstood to the other.

Do you experience this? What have you felt?

Have you talked about it with your friend?

In our friendships, there will be times when we hurt or disappoint one another. It's inevitable in our broken world. But with the grace of God firmly holding us, reminding us that he is the source of our true happiness, it is possible to nurture and sustain deep friendships throughout our lives.

Lifting the Veil

I have yet to meet the woman who always feels deeply connected to and loved by her friends. As women, we have days or seasons of sadness, feeling truly missed and hurt by our women friends. When you are feeling that way, invite Jesus into your sorrow. Ask him to come to you there. Feel your sadness. Ask him to comfort you and to speak to you in that place. Shed your tears. And then ask him to help you continue to love your friends wisely and well.

We are not made to live our lives alone. We are designed to live in relationship and share in the lives of other women. We need each other. God knows that. He will help us. We have only to ask and surrender, to wait, to hope, and in faith, to love. We must also repent.

We need to repent of our need to control and our insistence that people fill us.

Can you see the ways that you fall into this demand in your relationships? How?

Let us repent again and turn back to God. Again, ask him to reveal to you the truth that you are safe and secure in your relationship with him so you can risk being vulnerable with others and offer your true self.

Lifting the Veil

To love at all is to be vulnerable. Love anything, and your heart will certainly be wrung and possibly broken. If you want to make sure of keeping it intact, you must give your heart to no one, not even to an animal. Wrap it careful round with hobbies and little luxuries; avoid all entanglements; lock it up safe in the casket or coffin of your selfishness. But in that casket—safe, dark, motionless, airless—it will change. It will not be broken; it will become unbreakable, impenetrable, irredeemable . . . . The only place outside Heaven where you can be perfectly safe from all the dangers . . . of love is Hell.

—C. S. Lewis, The Four Loves

Ask God to help you become the kind of woman that others would long to have as a close friend. Ask him to reveal if there is anything hindering your friendships or set against them. (Past wounds, a strategy of self-protection that is backfiring, anything?)

We long for friendships. Just like our God, we long for intimacy. Our desire for relationship is a part of our glory. And our deep longing is part of the grace given to Eve to drive her to the River of Life.

Go to him now. In prayer. In Desire. In Worship.

CHAPTER ELEVEN

Warrior Princesses

"Me, a princess?"
"You are the legal heir."
"I never lead anyone."
"We will help you to be a princess, to rule. If you refuse to accept the throne then the kingdom will cease to exist as we know it."
—THE PRINCESS DIARIES

In God's name, we must fight them!
—JOAN OF ARC

Women are often portrayed in stories and tales as the "Damsel in Distress." We are the ones for whom men rise up and slay dragons. We are the "weaker sex"; said to faint at the sight of blood, needing to be spared the gory details of battle whether on the field or in the market place. We are the ones waiting in our flowing gowns for the knight to come and carry us away on the back of his white horse. And yes, there are days when a knight in shining armor would be most welcome. We do long to be fought for; loved enough to be courageously protected. But there is a mighty fierceness set in the hearts of women by God. This fierceness is true to who we are and what we are created to do.

Women are warriors, too.

Do you feel that to be true? In what way?

As always, let's ask for God's revelation and gentle guidance to come for us.

Dear Jesus, I love you. I need you. I come before you now, once again, as yours, asking for your help, your grace. My life is yours. My heart is yours. Would you please come and shine your light into my heart, my life, and my world that I might better understand myself and the spiritual world surrounding me. Help me to see, to understand, to repent, to forgive, to take a stand and to become. Jesus, I give you access to all of my heart. I invite you into every part. Come, Holy Spirit, have your way . . . that I might love you, God, more deeply, freely, and truly with all of my heart, soul, mind, and strength. In Jesus' name I pray. Amen.

Windows to Your Heart

We recommend you watch the scene we describe of Eowyn in the battle of the Pelenor Fields in *The Return of the King*—or another one like it. Women can be valiant warriors, too!

Now, go back over the chapter, skimming the pages. Did you highlight anything? What strikes you? What does it evoke in your heart?

What do you like about this chapter?

What did this chapter make you feel?

What did reading this chapter make you want to *do*?

What do you not like about this chapter? What are you struggling with?

Women Are Warriors, Too

We opened this chapter in the companion book by retelling the story from *The Lord of the Rings, Return of the King,* where Eowyn, disguised as a man, joins in the battle at Pelennor fields. She fights with fierce abandon and deadly skill. But when her uncle lays wounded at the mercy of the "Nazgul," she finds that fighting "as a man," will not avail her.

> "Begone, foul dwimmerlaik, lord of carrion! Leave the dead in peace!"
>
> A cold voice answered; "Come not between the Nazgûl and his prey! Or he will not slay thee in thy turn. He will bear thee away to the houses of lamentation, beyond all darkness, where thy flesh shall be devoured, and thy shriveled mind be left naked to the Lidless Eye."
>
> A sword rang as it was drawn. "Do what you will; but I will hinder it, if I may."
>
> In the battle that follows, the wraith is assured, cocky even. His strength is greater, his weapons more deadly. He boasts of an ancient prophecy, proclaiming,"Thou fool. No living man may hinder me!" And it is here that Éowyn is finally and fully victorious.
>
> It seemed that Dernhelm (Éowyn) laughed, and the clear voice was like the ring of steel. "But no living man am I! You look upon a woman. Éowyn I am, Éomund's daughter . . . Begone, if you be not deathless! For living or dark undead, I will smite you, if you touch him."

Éowyn removes her helmet and lets her hair fall free. She declares herself "no man" and fighting as a woman, slays her enemy. Something critically important is revealed in this story. Women are called to join in the Greatest Battle of all time—the battle being waged for the hearts of those around us. The human heart is the battlefield. The war is a deadly one; the results are devastating or glorious but always eternal. We are needed. There is much to be done. The hour is late. But we will only be victorious when we enter in with our feminine hearts—*when we battle as women.*

What rises up in your heart, if anything, when you read that "We are needed"?

At this point, what does battling "as a woman" mean to you?

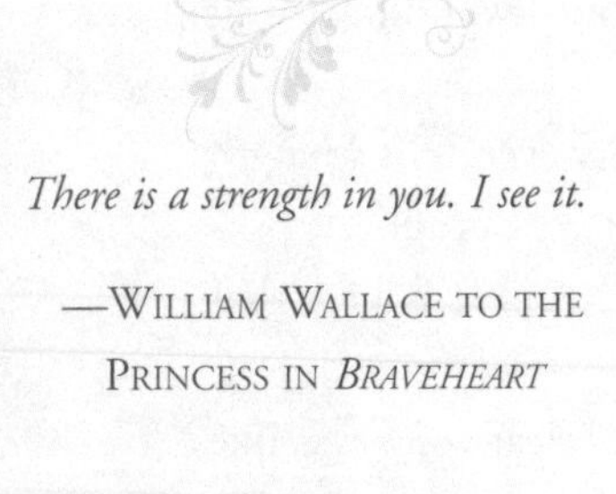

There is a strength in you. I see it.

—William Wallace to the Princess in *Braveheart*

Fighting Back

I shared about living with frequent dizzy spells. As it turns out, I didn't need to live with them. It is amazing what we will live with because we think it's normal when it absolutely is *not.*

Is spiritual warfare a new category for you to think in?

Do you or someone you know have any stories or experiences like mine?

How did you or those you know have to "take a stand"?

Is it possible that you are struggling with something that may have its source in the spiritual realm? What?

I saw, in gradual vision through my tears,
The sweet, sad years, the melancholy years,
Those of my own life, who by turns had flung
A shadow across me.

—Elizabeth Barrett Browning

Emotional Attacks

I know I am not alone in struggling with depression. Many women share this. Do you?

If yes, how have you sought relief from it?

Lifting the Veil

In this chapter I also shared that I had an abortion. (That was a really hard thing for me to share.) I know that I am not alone in this either. Let me first say that 1 John1:9 applies to this if it applies to anything.

If we confess our sins, he is faithful and just and will forgive us our sins and cleanse us from all unrighteousness.

But like me, perhaps you are having a hard time forgiving yourself. There is hope. Healing is possible. If abortion is part of your story, have you sought counseling yet?

Please, please do. If you don't know where to start, Focus on the Family can make a referral for someone in your area (1-800-A Family).

Body, Soul, and Spirit

We human beings are made up of three interwoven parts. As Paul says, "May God himself . . . sanctify you through and through. May your whole spirit, soul and body be kept blameless at the coming of our Lord Christ Jesus Christ" (1 Thess. 5:23 NKJV). We are body, soul, and spirit. Each part affects the others in a mysterious interplay of life.

Our bodies may be out of balance due to a chemical imbalance or a need for more sleep, exercise, or better diets. (It's wise, by the way, to find out if you are allergic to any types of food. Eating something you are allergic to can make you feel sluggish, depressed, ill, even give you awful mood swings.)

When we speak here of our souls, we are speaking of issues of our heart. Every person can benefit from counseling; either from a professional or a wise, well-trusted friend. The Holy Spirit, himself, is called our Counselor, and he too longs to meet us in the deep waters of our heart. We need to understand the story of our lives and receive the deep healing that God can bring.

Our spirit is that part of us in communion with God. ("But he who is joined to the Lord is one spirit with Him" (1 Cor. 6:17 NKJV). Spiritual struggles and spiritual healing affect every part of us. We all carry real wounds. Demons are attracted to our unhealed wounds like sharks are attracted to blood in the water. That spiritual attack makes our pain much, much worse.

In what areas are you struggling? Body, soul, or spirit? How?

Body:

Soul:

Spirit:

How may God be calling you to take a stand to fight for your freedom and healing?

We need to address all three aspects—body, soul, and spirit—in order to come more fully into healing. Far too many women will focus only on one or two aspects and not engage in the spiritual warfare that is swirling around us.

But if we would be free, we must.

Relational Attacks

Another common enemy that often is at work in women's relationships is a spirit of accusation. In our friendships, in our relationships with peers at work, and especially in our marriages, we often feel that we are a disappointment to others.

Do you know what I am talking about? Do you experience this? What difficulties are you having right now in your relationships?

Have you considered that the enemy of your soul may have a hand in this?

It would be good to find out. Expose the schemes of the enemy. Talk with your friend, your husband. Take a stand against the enemies' schemes and command him to leave. (This can feel a little weird at first, talking to the air and saying stuff like, "I bring the Cross of Christ against you. In Jesus' name I command you to leave.") Sometimes you have to be firm and pray several times. As Peter said, "firm in the faith" (1 Pet. 5:9 NKJV). But leave he does!

A Warring Bride

Ladies, you are the Bride of Christ, and the Bride of Christ is a warring bride.

We need to grow in our understanding and practice of spiritual warfare not only because we are being attacked, but because it is one of the primary ways that we grow in Christ. He uses spiritual warfare in our lives to strengthen our faith, to draw us closer to Him, to train us for the roles we are meant to play, to encourage us to play those roles, and to prepare us for our future at his side.

It is *not* that we are abandoned. Christ has not abandoned us.

It is *not* that we are alone. He will never leave us or forsake us.

It is *not* even up to us. The battle is the Lord's.

Jesus came through for us before we were even born. He fought for us before we even knew we needed him. He came, he died, he rose again *for us.* He was given all authority in heaven and on earth for us (Eph. 1:22). He has won the decisive victory against our Enemy. But we must apply it. Christianity is not a passive religion. It is an invasion of a Kingdom. We who are on the Lord's side must wield his victory. We must learn to enforce it. Women need to grow as warriors because we, too, were created to reign. God said of Eve as well as Adam, " . . . and let them rule" (Gen. 1:26 NKJV). And one day we will rule again (Matt. 25:21; Rev. 22:5). God allows spiritual warfare and uses it in our lives for our good. It is how we learn to grow in exercising our God-given spiritual authority as women.

Much of what he allows in your life is not for you to simply accept, but to *get you to rise up!*

What might that be in your life right now? A compulsion? An addiction? An illness? A struggle with depression, fear, feeling overwhelmed? (Yes, there is a spirit of overwhelmed. You can stand against it.)

Look up the following verses. (The Word of God is mighty in warfare. It is our sword!) What do they say?

1 John 3:8

John 10:10

Ephesians 6:10–17

Colossians 1:13–14

James 4:7

1 Peter 5:9

1 Timothy 6:12

2 Timothy 1:7

Matthew 16:21–23

Women are not meant to be helpless creatures. God has given us a fierceness that is holy and is to be used on behalf of others.

Warrior Princesses

What does a warrior princess look like? Think Joan of Arc. Think Mother Teresa. Think Esther. Think Mary of Bethany. Think Arwen. Think Éowyn. Think Deborah. Think Mary, Jesus' mother. Women who were wise, cunning, strong, beautiful, courageous, victorious, and very present. Present to God, present to others, and present—aware of—themselves.

Remember the story I shared from the retreat? After one session, we asked the women to go out and ask God for revelation and healing.

They were asking God to reveal the lies they had been living under, the sentences they had agreed with, and the vows they had made as a result. We had prayed God's grace and courage for them that they would renounce the lies, however true they felt, and invite God in to heal their wounded hearts and speak the truth.

God did speak to them. Take a few minutes now and quiet your soul. Ask God to reveal the enemy's lies to you. What are they?

Are you able to identify the enemy's key lies to your heart? If not, continue to ask God for revelation. It might help to ask yourself, "What do I always say to myself when I blow it?" "What do I hear when I think about stepping out in some new way—maybe attending to my beauty? Or cultivating a new friendship? Or pursuing a ministry, or dream?" A lot of what we "hear" inside our heads in not from us, dear sisters!

How has believing those accusations affected your life?

Have you broken your agreement with them? If not, DO! Whether you feel like it or not, you must break those agreements and make all agreements with God. It is time to renounce those lies. Even if they still feel true. Stop agreeing with Satan's verdict on your life. Make all agreements with God. Renounce the agreements with Satan. Out loud. Ask God to speak the truth to you.

Lifting the Veil

Your True Father loves to speak to you. He longs to tell you who you are and what he sees. And his voice is never condemning. Never. (Rom. 8:1.) Oh, he may need to convict you of sin, but the Lord's conviction leads to repentance, healing, freedom, and a grateful heart. Your heart spirals upward. On the other hand, the enemy's accusation fuels self-contempt and further hiding. Your heart spirals downward. It's a helpful way to tell the difference.

Women warriors are strong; yes, and they are also tender. There is mercy in them. There is vulnerability. In fact, offering a tender vulnerability can only be done by an incredibly strong woman, a woman rooted in Christ Jesus who knows whose she is and therefore knows who she is. Offering our hearts wisely, living in the freedom of God's love, inviting others to rest, alluring those in our lives to the heart of God, and responding to the heart of God in worship are some of the most powerful ways that a woman wars for her world. But she also puts on the full armor of God, daily, and takes her immovable stand against the powers of darkness.

Let us say it again. Your life is a Love Story set in the midst of a life-and-death battle. The beauty, the adventure, the intimacy—they are what are most real. But it is a battle to gain them, and a battle to keep them. A battle for your own heart and a battle for the hearts around you. "The LORD is a warrior; The LORD is his name." (Ex. 15:3 NKJV). Jesus fights on your behalf and on behalf of those you love. He asks you to join him.

Who would you love to see come into God's kingdom?

Who would you love to see healed of debilitating wounds?

Who do you long to see restored, becoming ever more whom God intended them to be?

Who do you want to see released to take their place in God's kingdom and fulfill his call on their lives?

What do *you* long to be free of?

Then you must take spiritual warfare seriously. First on behalf of your own heart and then mightily, for those you love.

Let's come to God in prayer.

> *Dearest Jesus, thank you for ransoming me. Father, thank you for rescuing me from the domain of darkness and transferring me into the kingdom of the Son you love. I am grateful beyond words to be yours. Please strengthen me for battle. Please reveal to me when I am under spiritual attack and teach me to take a stand against the enemy and to resist him. Even today, Jesus. Even now. In the name of Jesus Christ. Amen.*

Recommended Reading: We highly recommend that you obtain other resources to begin to learn more about your place in Christ, the authority he has given to you as a believer and how to take a stand against the enemy. Neil Anderson's *Victory Over the Darkness* and *The Bondage Breaker* are good places to start.

CHAPTER TWELVE

An Irreplaceable Role

If there is a real woman—even the trace of one—still there inside the grumbling, it can be brought to life again. If there's one wee spark under all those ashes, we'll blow it till the whole pile is red and clear.
—C. S. Lewis

Mary responded, "I am the Lord's servant, and I am willing to accept whatever he wants. May everything you have said come true."
—Luke 1:38 NLT

The story of *Cinderella* turns upon an invitation. *Our* story turns upon invitation. The King of kings invites us to choose him, to continue choosing him above all others and to risk joining him in the Great Dance, to offer what we have to offer, to live by faith, hope and love, and to play the irreplaceable, larger-than-we-are-comfortable-with role that is ours to play.

Let's pray!

Dear Jesus, I love you. I need you. I come before you now, once again, as yours, asking for your help, your grace, your courage. My life is yours. My heart is yours. Would you please come and shine your light into the depths of my heart that I might understand myself better;, the dreams and desires that you have placed there, and come to know your healing and your presence more deeply. Help me to remember what I need to remember. Help me to see, to understand, to repent, to forgive, and to become. Jesus, I give you access to all of my heart. I invite you into every part. Help me understand what it is you are inviting me to because I desire to respond to your invitation with holy faith. Come, Holy Spirit, have your way . . . that I might love you, God, more deeply and truly with all of my heart, soul, mind, and strength. In Jesus' name I pray. Amen.

Windows to Your Heart

Finding our place in God's story (which is what we mean by finding your calling) is a process of discovery. We believe that God writes the destiny of our lives upon our hearts—in the form of our dreams and desires.

In the book of Acts, it says that "David . . . served God's purpose in his own generation" (13:36 NKJV). That's what it looked like from the outside. David accomplished his life's mission. But how did it feel on the inside? What was that like for David? "You have granted [me] the desire of [my] heart" (Ps. 21:2 NKJV). In other words, the deepest desires of David's heart were the very same things that God wanted him to do! Isn't that beautiful?

Uncovering those desires and dreams—and recovering ones that have been lost—is a crucial part to finding our place in God's story. God will send us all sorts of things to stir us to remember. Sometimes it's a long-forgotten memory, a photograph. Other times it's a story you hear about someone's life, and you find yourself longing to be or do the same thing. Another reason we love stories and movies so is that we have found they stir in us our heart's desires. Quite often you'll find that you identify with a certain character in a movie you love. The reason why is that their life is speaking to you about something written deep on your heart about your life!

As you let yourself dream and wonder, recall those things that have stirred your heart—memories, photographs, stories and movies and characters you most deeply love, identify with, long to be. Then ask God why—ask him to speak to you about that.

Now, go back over the chapter, skimming the pages. What does it evoke in your heart?

What do you like about this chapter?

What do you not like about it? What are you struggling with?

What does playing your vital role as an *ezer* look like in your life?

What do you want it to look like in the future?

What would that require?

Invited

How gracious that God comes to us with invitation. As a woman, you don't need to arrange, you don't need to make it happen. You only need to respond.

Do you have a sense of what it is that God is inviting you to? What?

Mary, the mother of Jesus' life, also turned upon invitation. What was God's invitation to Mary? How did she respond?

The invitations of our Prince come to us in all sorts of ways. Your heart itself, as a woman, is an invitation. An invitation delivered in the most intimate and personalized way. Your Lover has written something on your heart. It is a call to find a life of Romance and to protect that love affair as your most precious treasure.

What love affair are we speaking of?

His invitation is a call to cultivate the beauty you hold inside and to unveil your beauty on behalf of others. And it is a call to adventure, to become the *ezer* the world desperately needs you to be.

Are you beginning to believe that you possess a beauty to unveil? A beauty the world needs?

The Power of a Woman's Life

When the history of the world is finally told rightly—one of the great joys when we reach the Wedding Feast of the Lamb—it will be as clear as day that women have been essential to every great move of God upon this earth.

Can you think of some that we did not mention? Biblically? Historically?

From the beginning, Eve was God's gift to the world—his *ezer kenegdo* for us. History is still unfolding and your existence on this earth as a woman is proof that you have an irreplaceable role to play. You are a woman, are you not? An *ezer kenegdo* to your core. Your lingering disbelief (may it be fading away) that anything important hangs on your life is only evidence of the long assault on your heart by the one who knows who you could be and fears you.

Your feminine heart is an invitation by your Creator. To what? To play an irreplaceable role in his Story. Isn't that what your Lover wrote there? Some dream, some desire, something so core to who you are it almost hurts to think of it. The very longing is such a part of your being it's scary even to give it a voice.

What has God written on your heart? What dreams, what desires, what longings?

YOUR IRREPLACEABLE ROLE

Our true places as women in God's Story are as diverse and unique as wildflowers in a field. No two look quite the same. But we all share certain spheres of influence to which we are called to be an *ezer* in our relationships, in the body of Christ, and in the world.

In Your Relationships

Eve is God's relational specialist given to the world to keep relationship a priority. In fact, we learn from the Trinity that relationship is the most important thing in the universe. You have an irreplaceable role in your relationships.

Who are the key people in your relationships?

What does it look like for you to offer your beauty, your fierce devotion, and your love in your relationships?

How do they need you to be their *ezer*? What would keep you from offering it to them?

Do your relationships feel *opposed* at times? How?

Satan knew that to take out Adam, all he had to do was take out Eve.

All the Enemy has to do to destroy people's lives is to get them isolated, a lamb separated from the flock. To do this he removes the *ezers* in their life. He makes a woman feel like, "What do I have to offer, really? They're probably doing fine."

Have you ever felt that with someone, and it kept you from reaching out to them? Did you ever find out later that during that time they really needed you? We have got to stop believing the schemes of the enemy. You are needed. You have been sent by the Trinity on behalf of love, of relationships. You must fight for them.

What does that make you feel? Who do you want to fight for?

In the Body of Christ

Your life is also part of a larger movement, a mystical fellowship, the kingdom of God advancing here on earth. That fellowship of the Ransomed and being Restored—that is an amazing fellowship to be a part of. To be sure, it's messy. Have you noticed in Paul's letters to the young church how often he has to intervene in relationships?

Does that encourage you?

The fellowship of Christ is messy, because it, too, is *opposed.* And here, you have an irreplaceable role to play.

We haven't time here to address the issues surrounding "the proper role of women" in the church. That would also take a book in itself. However, we do believe it is far more helpful to start with Design—with what God designed a woman to be and to offer.

God desires that wherever and however you offer yourself to the body of Christ, you'll have the protection of good men over you. Not to hold you back, but to set you free as a woman. Issues of headship and authority are intended for the *benefit* of women, not their suppression. You know how dangerous it can be to try and come alive as a truly feminine woman. Right?

What do you want to offer in the body of Christ?

Do you know your gifting? Your calling? What is it?

The role of women in the church is much larger than many of us have been taught or allowed to play. We need women to rise up, to follow Jesus where he leads them and to play their irreplaceable role in his kingdom.

When we speak of your irreplaceable role within the body of Christ, we're talking about the true fellowship of those whose hearts are captured for Jesus, who have become his intimate allies. You want to offer yourself to those who thirst for what you have. If it's not wanted where you are, ask Jesus what he wants you to do.

If you are called, God will make a way. Either where you are or through a change of circumstances. Follow your Lover; respond to his invitations. With him, there is no stopping you.

Do you need to change your situation—find a true fellowship where your heart is wanted—and where you are among those who want what you want?

In the World

Stepping further out into your farthest sphere of influence, you have something essential to offer the World. It may be in the form of a notable career. It may be a hidden life, well-lived. Some women are called to the marketplace.

Are you? In what way? How is God calling you to play your irreplaceable role there?

The crucial issue is this: It is as a *woman* you must live there. Do not be naïve. The World is still deeply marred by the Fall. Men still dominate in many sinful ways (remember the curse). Women who "make it" there tend to be dominating and controlling (remember Fallen Eve). The Evil One holds sway over the World and its systems (1 John 5:19). In the World you must be as cunning as a Rahab, an Esther, a Tamar. You must walk wisely. You must not let them shape you into their view of what a woman is. You'll end up a man. What you have to offer is as a woman. Uniquely feminine.

If you have a role in the marketplace, what would it look like for you to recover more of your feminine heart there? To be a woman there?

What Is Written on Your Heart

As I said earlier, the invitations of Jesus come to us in many ways. Sometimes they come through a circumstance, an opportunity that opens before us. Sometimes they come through other people, who see something in us that we may not yet see, and they invite us to step forth in some way. But God's invitations ultimately are matters of the heart. They come through our passions, those desires set deep within us.

How have God's invitations come to you in the past?

How are they coming to you now?

What is it you yearn to see happen? How do you long to make the world a better place?

What makes you so angry you nearly see red? What brings you to tears?

Lifting the Veil

"The place that God calls us is that place where the world's deep hunger and our deep desire meet."—Frederick Buechner

You will find that as God restores your heart and sets you free, you will recover long lost passions, long-forsaken dreams. You'll find yourself drawn to some vision for making the world a better place. Those emerging desires are invitations to bring your heart to your Lover and ask him to clarify, to deepen, to speak to you about how and when and with whom.

What desires are emerging within you? Any long lost passions being re-kindled?

Do Not Give Way to Fear

Of course this is scary. Responding to the invitations of Jesus often feels like the riskiest thing we've ever done. The life of the friends of God is a life of profound risk. The risk of loving others. The risk of stepping out and offering, speaking up and following our God-given dreams. The risk of playing the irreplaceable role that is ours to play. Of course it is hard. If it were easy, you'd see lots of women living this way.

So let's come back then to what Peter said when he urged women to offer their beauty to others in love. This is the secret of femininity unleashed:

Do not give way to fear.
—1 Peter 3:6 NKJV

The reason we fear to step out is because we know that it might not go well.

Would you say this is an understatement? What is it you fear most?

How can we live lives without fear? (1 Peter 2:21–23)

What is God calling you to risk? What is he calling you to offer? Where is he asking you to step out in faith that feels scary to you?

We need you. The body of Christ needs you. The world needs you.

We don't get to wait to offer our lives until we have our acts together. We don't get that luxury. If we did, would anyone ever feel like offering anything??? God asks us to be vulnerable. He invites us to share and give in our weaknesses. He wants us to offer the beauty that he has given us even when we are keenly aware that it is not all that we wish it were. He wants us to trust him. How it turns out is no longer the point. Living in this way, as a woman alive, is a choice we make because it is the woman we want to be. It is our loving response to our Lover's invitation.

Be Present

> Now we should live when the pulse of life is strong. Life is a tenuous thing—fragile, fleeting. Don't wait for tomorrow. Be here now! Be here now! Be here now!

What does the above quote mean to you?

Where would it be good for you to be more *present*? To offer your presence?

To live as an authentic, ransomed, and redeemed woman means to be real and present, in this moment. If we continue to hide, much will be lost. We cannot have intimacy with God or anyone else if we stay hidden and offer only who we think we ought to be or what we believe is wanted. We cannot play the *ezer* role we were meant to play if we remain bound by shame and fear, presenting only to the world the face we have learned is safe.

What have we to offer, really, other than who we are and what God has been pouring into our lives? It was not by accident that you were born; it was not by chance that you have the desires you do. The Victorious Trinity has planned on your being here now, "for such a time as this" (Esth. 4:14 NKJV). We need you.

> Jesus knew that the Father had put all things under his power, *and that he had come from God and was returning to God;* so he got up from the meal, took off his outer clothing, and wrapped a towel around his waist. After that, he poured water into a basin and began to wash his disciples' feet, drying them with the towel that was wrapped around him.
>
> —John 13:3–5 NKJV, emphasis added

Jesus knew who he was. God wants you to know who you are as well.

So, who *are* you? How does God see you? How does he feel about you?

Is he captivated by your beauty?

Does he love you?

Does he need you?

What does he want from you?

What is he inviting you to?

Remember the scene I describe at the end of *Anna and the King*? Put yourself in as Anna. Put Jesus in as the King.

Jesus is extending his hand to you. He is inviting you to dance with him. He asks, "May I have this dance every day of your life?" His gaze is fixed on you. He is captivated by your beauty. He is smiling. He cares nothing of the opinion of others. He is standing. He will lead. He waits for your response.

Take some time here. What is your heart's response to Jesus?

"My lover spoke and said to me,
'Arise, my darling,
my beautiful one, and come with me.'"
—Song of Songs 2:10 NKJV

Closing Thoughts

Okay. We've come to the end of this *Guided Journal.* Any favorite chapters?

Anything you want to linger with for awhile?

Any chapters you'd like to revisit or go deeper into?

There is always more. More healing. More life. More repentance. More freedom. More of Jesus. More faith, more hope, more love. And dear sister, that is very good news. We are on this journey together. A journey with Jesus to become increasingly transformed into his beautiful likeness; increasingly *his.*

May he bless you and keep you. May he make his face to shine upon you. And give you peace.

Rest in his love. He is enough.

Other Books from John Eldredge

Captivating. John Eldgredge and his wife, Stasi, show women how to reveal their three core desires—to be romanced, to play an irreplaceable role in a grand adventure, and to unveil beauty—and encourage them to restore their feminine heart. In the style of *Wild at Heart,* women are shown the possibilities their dreams can afford, and men are given a glimpse into a woman's soul, where they can see the strength and beauty God placed there for a reason.

Hardcover Edition—ISBN 0-7852-6469-8
Abridged Audio on 3 CDs—ISBN 0-7852-0909-3
Spanish Edition *(Cautivante)*—ISBN 0-8811-3278-0

● ● ●

Epic. In this retelling of the gospel in four acts, John Eldredge presents God not only as the author of life, but also as the actor in a story where the "plot" reaches the depths of our souls. Now you, too, can discover your role in the drama. This book shows how our hearts long for great drama and why the gospel is truly epic.

Hardcover Edition—ISBN 0-7852-6531-7
Spanish Edition *(Majestuoso)*—ISBN 0-8811-3808-8
Unabridged Audio on 2 CDs—ISBN 0-7852-0910-7
Epic Discussion Guide—ISBN 1-4185-0015-1

•••

Waking the Dead. In *Waking the Dead,* John Eldredge shows how God restores your heart, your true humanity, and sets you free. There are four streams, Eldredge says, through which you can discover the abundant life: Walking with God, Receiving His Intimate Counsel, Deep Restoration, and Spiritual Warfare. And once the "eyes of your heart" are opened, you will embrace three eternal truths: Things are not what they seem; This is a world at war; and You have a crucial role to play. A battle is raging. And it is a battle for your heart.

Hardcover—ISBN 0-7852-6553-8
Abridged Audio in 3 CDs—ISBN 0-7852-6299-7

•••

A Guidebook to Waking the Dead. In a style similar to *The Journey of Desire Journal and Guidebook,* Eldredge and Craig McConnell lead you on a journey toward a restored heart, true humanity, and ultimate freedom.

ISBN 0-7852-6309-8

•••

Wild at Heart. Every man was once a boy. And every little boy has dreams, big dreams. But what happens to those dreams when they grow up? In *Wild at Heart,* John Eldredge invites men to recover their masculine heart, defined in the image of a passionate God. And he invites women to discover the secret of a man's soul and to delight in the strength and wildness men were created to offer.

Hardcover—ISBN 0-7852-6883-9
Abridged Audio in 3 CDs—ISBN 0-7852-6298-9

Abridged Audio in 2 Cassettes—ISBN 0-7852-6498-1
Spanish Edition *(Salvaje de Corazón)*—ISBN 0-8811-3716-2

●●●

Wild at Heart Field Manual. Abandoning the format of workbooks-as-you-know-them, the *Wild at Heart Field Manual* will take you on a journey through which you will receive permission to be what God designed you to be—dangerous, passionate, alive, and free. Filled with questions, exercises, personal stories from readers, and wide-open writing spaces to record your "field notes," this book will lead you on a journey to discover the masculine heart that God gave you.

ISBN 0-7852-6574-0

●●●

Wild at Heart: A Band of Brothers. Five friends. Eight days. No scripts. Here's what it looks like to live the message of *Wild at Heart* in a band of real brothers. John and his band of brothers spent eight days shooting this series on a ranch in Colorado. Horses. Rappelling. White-water rafting. Fly-fishing. And some of the most honest conversation you will ever hear from men. This is not a scripted instructional video. It is real life and conversation shared with the cameras rolling. If you're looking for more, this is the next step in the *Wild at Heart* adventure for you and your band of brothers. The Multi-Media Facilitator's Kit includes John's best-selling *Wild at Heart* hardcover book; the *Wild at Heart Field Manual;* the *Wild at Heart Facilitator's Guide;* the video teaching series available either in VHS or DVD format; and a media kit to help you get the word out so others can join your band of brothers.

VHS ISBN 1-4002-0087-3
DVD ISBN 1-4002-0086-5

• • •

The Wild at Heart Journal. This rugged, leather-bound guided journey will help men explore their hearts and journal their adventures. This includes totally different material from that found in the *Field Manual.*

ISBN 0-8499-5763-X

• • •

The Journey of Desire. Author Dan Allender calls *The Journey of Desire* "a profound and winsome call to walk into the heart of God." This life-changing book picks up where *The Sacred Romance* leaves off and continues the journey. In it, John Eldredge invites you to abandon resignation, to rediscover your God-given desires, and to search again for the life you once dreamed of.

Hardcover Edition—ISBN 0-7852-6882-0
Trade Paper Edition—ISBN 0-7852-6716-6

• • •

The Journey of Desire Journal and Guidebook. John Eldredge, with Craig McConnell, offers a unique, thought-provoking, and life-recapturing workbook, which invites you to rediscover your God-given desire and to search again for the life you once dreamed of. Less of a workbook and more of a flowing journal, this book includes personal responses to questions from John and Craig.

ISBN 0-7852-6640-2

• • •

The Sacred Romance. This life-changing book by Brent Curtis and John Eldredge has guided hundreds of thousands of readers from a busyness-based religion to a deeply felt relationship with the God who woos you. As you draw closer to Him, you must choose to let go of other "less-wild lovers," such as perfectionistic drivenness and self-indulgence, and embark on your own journey to recover the lost life of your heart and with it the intimacy, beauty, and adventure of life with God.

Trade Paper Edition—ISBN 0-7852-7342-5
Special Collector's Edition (Hardcover)—ISBN 0-7852-6723-9
Abridged Audio in 2 Cassettes—ISBN 0-7852-6786-7
Spanish Edition *(El Sagrado Romance)*—ISBN 0-8811-3648-4

• • •

The Sacred Romance Workbook and Journal. John Eldredge offers a guided journey of the heart featuring exercises, journaling, and the arts to usher you into an *experience*—the recovery of your heart and the discovery of your life as part of God's great romance.

JOHN ELDREDGE
Author of The Journey of Desire and Coauthor of The Sacred Romance
WILD at HEART
DISCOVERING THE SECRET of A MAN'S SOUL

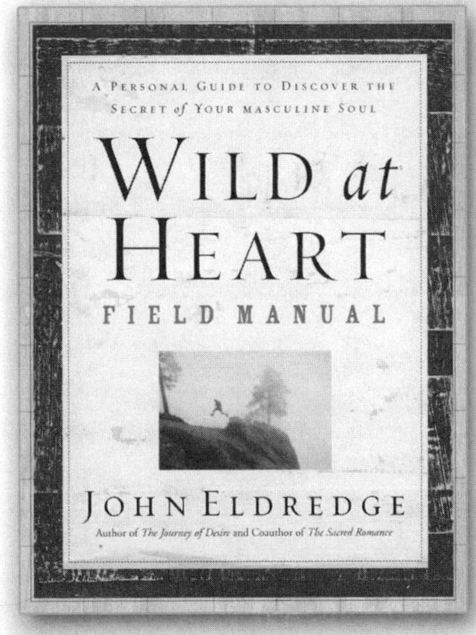
A PERSONAL GUIDE TO DISCOVER THE SECRET of YOUR MASCULINE SOUL
WILD at HEART
FIELD MANUAL
JOHN ELDREDGE
Author of The Journey of Desire and Coauthor of The Sacred Romance

We want to hear from you! Please visit us at www.nelsonimpact.com and send us your comments about this book. Thank you.

NELSON IMPACT
A Division of Thomas Nelson Publishers
Since 1798

www.thomasnelson.com